ESCAPE the PAYCHECK to PAYCHECK TRAP

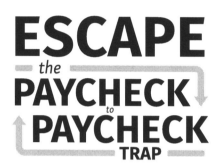

ESCAPE the PAYCHECK to PAYCHECK TRAP

The Ultimate Plan to Get Out of Debt and Supersize Your Savings

Tina Antrim

Published by Life Change Publishing

ISBN: 978-1-7338538-0-4 (paperback)

ISBN: 978-1-7338538-1-1 (ebook)

Unless otherwise noted, the stories in this book are based on a collection of client experiences. Most names and identifying information have been changed to protect the person's privacy.

Disclaimer: The information in this book is designed to provide helpful information on the subjects discussed based on the author's opinions. It is not intended to be a substitute for legal or financial advice for your specific situation.

Cover and Interior Design: Jerry Dorris, AuthorSupport.com

First Printing April 2019 / Printed in the United States of America

This book is dedicated to
everyone who feels embarrassed,
ashamed, and fearful about their financial situation.

It is dedicated to those who are tired of
worrying about how to pay for the next crisis
or unexpected expense.

And it is dedicated to those who desire to give
generously, save abundantly, and spend without remorse.

This book is dedicated to YOU!

Contents

Introduction

"I'm tired of living paycheck to paycheck."

"I know I should be saving but there just isn't any money left."

"I'm so embarrassed / ashamed about my financial situation."

"I make really good money. I can't figure out why I never seem to have any!"

"I feel guilty that I can't give more to my church."

"I don't think I will ever be able to retire."

Do any of these statements ring true for you? I have personally said every single one of them, and I hear them from my clients all the time. So, if they resonate with you, you're not alone. It doesn't matter if you are male or female, young or old, make $30,000 or over six figures. The majority of us struggle with money issues.

How are you supposed to pay your bills, save for emergencies, take family vacations, save for your kids' college, pay for larger emergencies, and oh yeah, put a little away for retirement? It's a lot to figure out. And there is *always* an emergency, right? The car gets a flat tire, child gets sick or hurt, washer stops working, roof needs replaced, spouse loses their job, and the list goes on.

It can be a little overwhelming! And if you don't think you're "good with money," then it can feel downright terrifying.

Recently, I was at the library browsing book titles. Just as there are loads of books on how to live a healthier life, you can find dozens – maybe even hundreds – of books on and how to manage money. For every health issue you can think of, someone has written a book about how to deal with it. For personal finance, there are a multitude of books on budgeting, managing money, investing, becoming a millionaire, and more. If you search for these kinds of books online, the number increases exponentially.

In addition, there are all kinds of resources available to help you: fitness centers, financial advisor firms, trainers, workshops and classes, blogs, magazine articles, podcasts, and television shows.

And yet, despite all of this information, many are still overweight and most Americans are in debt and living paycheck to paycheck. And I ask myself "Why?"

Why are so many people struggling to maintain a healthy lifestyle?

Why are so many people living paycheck to paycheck or just getting by?

Why are so many people drowning in fear and insecurity because of their financial situation?

Why are so many people not able to even think about retiring?

Here's what I know. I'm a smart person, and I'm betting you are as well. However, that doesn't mean I always make the best decisions. For example, I know that I'm supposed to eat more fruits and vegetables and less pasta and pizza (nearly impossible for me!) and exercise more. Financially, I'm supposed to spend less and save more. But, I admit that I don't always do what I know I should do. I crave my carbs and spending money is just sometimes a lot more fun than saving it.

As a financial coach and educator, I have discovered that regardless of how much information is available, many of us still struggle with our finances. I have worked with many men and women who are broken, overwhelmed, ashamed, and scared for what the future holds for them. Things are not working out the way they expected, and they are lost and confused. The stress is causing marriages to suffer, relationships with family and friends to fracture, physical and emotional health to decline, and employment to be jeopardized.

I've been there! I'm a spender at heart and a recovering shopaholic. I did just about everything wrong with money that one can do. I lived paycheck to paycheck for many years believing that was how everyone lived and that was how it's supposed to be. Thankfully, I finally figured out that's *not* how we're called to live our financial lives, and it *doesn't* have to be that way, *if* we don't want it to. Notice that I said, "*IF we don't want it to.*" We often tell ourselves that we should probably save more or get out of debt or give more. And we really think it's a good idea. But, do you notice that something always gets in the way of doing that? Ultimately, it *sounds* like a good idea, but when it comes to making decisions to do those things, we often choose to keep doing what we've always done. It's what we're comfortable with.

I started thinking about this gap between what we want and know we should do and what we actually do. I thought about my clients who come to me stressed and filled with anxiety about their financial situations. I dreamed about what it would be like if everyone could escape the paycheck-to-paycheck trap to have positive monthly cash flow and financial freedom. And I decided to become one more voice that will hopefully make a difference in people changing their money habits, stories, and situations.

In *Escape the Paycheck to Paycheck Trap*, I endeavor to answer those "why" questions and show you how to close the gap. Through my story and the stories of others, I hope you will finally be able to create a plan that promotes confidence and peace and gives you strength to move forward one step at a time. While reading this book, you will explore your own story around money, discover your spending triggers (those areas keeping you stuck in the trap), establish achievable goals that will help you get out of debt and supersize your savings, and design a spending plan you can actually stick to.

This book is for you if you are tired of living paycheck to paycheck or are done with having "just enough," wondering where the money goes each month, and being stressed about your financial situation all the time. It is for you if you're ready to make a change and ready to create a plan for YOUR financial freedom. I hope it will *challenge your thinking, motivate you to action, and change your lifestyle.*

So, are you willing to be open to some new ways of thinking about money? Are you ready to become financially fit? Even more so, are you ready to *step out of your complacency* and start making some changes? Then you are in the right place.

To help you escape the paycheck-to-paycheck trap, I have included *Planning Your Escape* activities for you to complete as you move through the book. It is up to you whether you do them, but I believe that completing them will take you to the next level even faster. At the very least, write some general thoughts down as you read and then you can go back and fill in more details later.

At the end of most chapters, you will find a special section that offers a spiritual perspective on that topic. I am a Christian, and the Bible and God's principles around money have played a profound impact on how and why I changed my financial situation. I would not have the freedom that I have today without His grace and blessings. Even if you do not identify with the Christian faith, these sections will still be of value to you, helping you make a deeper connection with your money and your faith.

The time to take control is now. You've got this, and I will be with you each step of the way. Find a quiet place to relax for a while and let's get started.

PART I

Prepare Your Escape

CHAPTER 1

Acknowledging the Pain

I came home exhausted from work one night. I was working full-time as a youth director for a local church and also had a part-time job at a bookstore in the mall. I enjoyed both positions, but it was really taking a toll on me mentally and physically. Still, I had to keep both jobs in order to pay my bills, especially the credit card debt that I had accumulated. I stopped to get my mail as was my normal routine and flinched at the two credit card statements that were there. Didn't I just get a statement from them? I trudged up to my apartment feeling even more exhausted and distressed as I thought about having to open the mail and see the late fees and interest. No matter how hard I tried to pay down those credit card bills, they never seemed to go away.

I felt so alone. No one knew what I was going through. I didn't tell family or any of my friends because I was too embarrassed. Too ashamed. I felt guilty for all of the dumb decisions that I had made with my money. To relieve those negative emotions, I often went shopping. And of course, I had to buy something because what's the use of going shopping if you're not going to buy something, right? The initial euphoria of finding a great deal (and just spending money in general) would give way to more shame and guilt.

I was a fraud. I acted like I had money. I spent like I had money. I plopped my credit card down on the cashier's desk with a big smile. But the sad reality was that I could barely pay my bills. I was stuck in a trap of living beyond paycheck to paycheck, meaning I was living beyond what my paycheck would cover. There were times that my bills were paid with a credit card because I didn't have enough money coming in to even pay for rent and utilities.

I remember getting a phone call early one morning from someone who told me I had just won a free trip for two to the Bahamas. All I had to pay was transportation and attend a meeting one day while we were there. I don't know if it was because the guy had woken me up and my brain was still foggy or because I had to make a decision in an instant, but I said YES, sign me up for this free trip. After giving them my contact and credit card information, I hung up the phone thinking, "What the heck did I just do? Did I just fall into a scam?" But it was a free vacation; I had to do it. Not long after, I realized that it wasn't going to be free. I would have to pay for the flight, the hotel cost in Miami (the hotel in the Bahamas was paid for as well as the one-day cruise there and back), a rental car, and some food. How did I pay for it? You guessed it. I opened up a new credit card that was 0% interest for twelve months. I went on that vacation with a friend from high school and had a great time. We even got out of the time share talk (you knew that's what the trip was about, right?) because it got canceled.

Reality slapped me in the face a month later when I got that credit card statement in the mail. I spent HOW MUCH?? Regret and fear swept over me. What was I going to do? I already had debt that I was trying to pay off. Now, I had more. What happened? Would I never learn my lesson? Why couldn't I stop spending money that I didn't have? What was wrong with me?

I run into people all the time with these same stories and same thoughts and fears. If I asked you how you feel about your financial situation right now, what would you say? What are the first words that come to your mind?

If you said *content, peaceful, confident, freedom* or anything else like that, then congratulations and that is fantastic. If, however, you said *shame, fearful, guilty, embarrassed, worried, stressed*, or something similar, then please know you are not alone. In fact, you probably fall into the majority. Many Americans are stressed about their current financial situation and fearful about the future, even those who have accumulated some level of wealth. A 2018 Planning & Progress Study conducted by Northwestern Mutual found that money was the dominant source of stress (44%), dramatically outpacing stress from personal relationships and work.[1] Still, it can feel like you are on an island all by yourself when you look around and everyone else *seems* to be doing better than you.

Back in 2007-2008, when the housing bubble burst followed by the Great Recession, the world was thrown into financial and emotional chaos. Many people lost their homes, their jobs, their businesses, their investments, and their stability. People who thought they were financially free and living the good life got smacked with a jolt of sudden insecurity. Although I didn't lose my job or my home, I remember watching my investment accounts take a tumble. It was frightening and very stressful. Like others, I wondered how long it would last and how much more turmoil would take place.

After what seemed like a lifetime, the economy slowly started to pick up. According to the National Bureau of Economic Research, the recession officially ended in June 2009.[2] In the near decade since, the stock market has had record high returns, housing has bounced back and wealth has been restored for many households. Some are financially better now than they were before the crash, even if there are a few emotional scars left. For others, those first few years during and immediately after the recession are still embedded in their psyche, and many have still not fully recovered financially. They vividly remember the fear, the loss, and the stress, and it is keeping some frozen and unable to move forward.

One crisis. Two very different outcomes.

When the recession began, my biggest fear was losing money in my investments because I knew it would take time to recoup the difference. Thankfully, I was no longer living paycheck to paycheck. I had a steady job with high seniority, so I wasn't too worried about losing it (even though I recognized that anything could happen). But looking around and hearing the heartbreaking stories of people who were experiencing great losses prompted me to make some decisions. They included a dedication to pay off my house as soon as possible and increase my savings. I also committed to reevaluate and determine my priorities – what was most important to me – especially in the area of spending.

Maybe you made some of your own commitments and reevaluations during that time. Do you remember what they were? Isn't it funny how the passing of time can make us forget things or at least put us in a frame of mind where we don't think about that crisis as often? It's not a bad thing. In fact, it's a good thing when you're trying to heal from pain and tragedy. It's not healthy to stay frozen in time feeling hurt, betrayed, and lost. We've got to move forward. I know it's not easy, and honestly, I think it's good to remember some of it. Depending on what it was, we can learn from those experiences.

A decade removed from the recession crisis – I see people moving on and feeling a little better about their financial situations. Many have found new jobs, new homes, and more money. They are feeling more confident about the economy, so spending is picking up. That's all great, but I'm also hearing and seeing something else. People are going back to their same patterns and habits from the pre-recession days. They are spending more and saving less. Some are now dipping into that nice savings cushion they had built to buy stuff that they want (not need). This is where that passage of time numbing the pain we once felt can jeopardize our prior commitments and plans. We forget why we made those commitments now that things are better. We start making decisions that contradict what we initially set out to do and that seemed so important at the time.

So, how about you? Where do you stand now? Do you find yourself unable to fall asleep or waking up in the middle of the night worrying about your financial situation? Do you break out in a cold sweat when you get ready to check the mailbox? Have you put all those overdue bills into a drawer "to get to later"? Are you constantly trying to figure out a way to increase your cash flow and find more money? Do you feel like there is something wrong with you because you just can't seem to get a handle on this money thing? Do you make really good money but just can't seem to save any of it or have anything left for fun?

If you're nodding your head and quietly saying yes to any or all of these questions, take a deep breath. I've already told you that I've been there and answered yes to *all* of those questions. That is why it was so easy for me to come up with them. I often had to take a step back and breathe. So, take that deep breath now . . . and now again, nice and slow. Deep breathing is an automatic stress reliever. Whether you're frustrated with your kids, spouse, coworkers, other drivers on the road who don't know how to drive or your money situation, taking a few slow, deep breaths can keep you from saying or doing something that you might later regret.

Know this – *you are not defined by your financial situation*! No matter how bad things may be for you financially right now, it does not define who you are. You are not defined by your debt, your lack of savings, your inability to stick with a budget, and so forth. Got it? I want you to write on a piece of paper, "I am not defined by my [fill in the blank]," and post it where you will see it, to remind you of this important message.

Now, are you ready to take some action, change direction, and stop living paycheck to paycheck? The next chapter dives into what this paycheck-to-paycheck lifestyle is all about and why we can't seem to escape its trap. But first, do the activities at the end of this chapter.

Spiritual Perspective

When I was in debt and living paycheck to paycheck, I often felt convicted and guilty about my financial situation. I knew that I wasn't being faithful in my finances and was taking advantage of the resources that God had blessed me with. But, for a long time that guilt wasn't enough to change my habits.

I think most believers really want to be better stewards and managers of their money. We have a desire to give to our church and to people in need. We don't want to be slaves to our debt. But we're no different than anyone else when it comes to our emotions and tendencies to overspend, and that can prevent us from making good decisions with our money.

As Christians, I do think we have an increased responsibility to manage our finances wisely because we know and believe that all we have comes from God. Yes, we work really hard and want to be rewarded for that, but even the work we do and the physical and mental capacities that we have to do that work comes from Him. That responsibility weighed heavily on me as I realized how I had so often squandered what He had blessed me with. My desire to be a better Christian and witness was a big part of what challenged me to take a hard look at the choices I was making around money and commit to making some changes.

There are well over two thousand verses in the Bible that talk about money matters. One of my favorite passages is 1 Chronicles 29:12-16 where King David acknowledges this very idea that everything we have comes from God. He says, "Wealth and honor come from you . . . everything comes from you . . . comes from your hand, and all of it belongs to you." Three times he acknowledges this!

Why is this important? Because while everything belongs to God, we are still responsible for what He has entrusted to us and that includes money.

Planning Your Escape

1. When you think about your current financial situation, what words come to mind for you? Think of as many as you can and complete the following sentence.
   I feel:

2. What mistakes do you think you have made with money that have contributed to your financial situation?

3. What things have you done well in regards to managing your money?

4. What commitments or decisions did you make around money in the past several years that have gone by the wayside (save more, pay off debt, begin investing, increase investments, etc.)?

5. What got in the way of keeping those commitments?

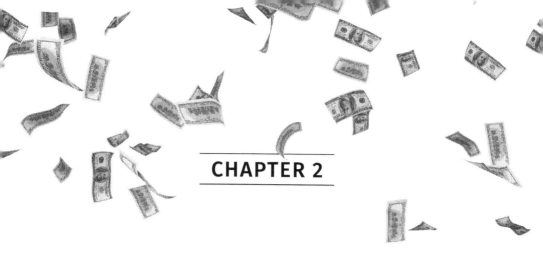

CHAPTER 2

Paycheck to Paycheck

According to a 2017 survey by Career Builder, it is estimated that 78% of full-time workers in the United States are living paycheck to paycheck.[3] What does it mean to live paycheck to paycheck? According to *Investopedia*, "Paycheck to paycheck is an expression used to describe an individual who would be unable to meet financial obligations if unemployed because his or her salary is predominantly devoted to expenses." [4] *Merriam-Webster* defines it this way: "to spend all of the money from one paycheck before receiving the next paycheck." Does this describe you? If it does, you are certainly not alone. Even people bringing in a healthy income often have the majority of their paycheck going to expenses.

Now, those expenses could be primarily fixed and necessary, such as your mortgage or rent, utilities, insurance, and debt repayments, including an auto loan or school loan. Or they could include ones that are variable (or discretionary), which can usually be reduced or eliminated. Eating out, cell phone bills, clothing (beyond essentials), hobbies, gym memberships and vacations fall into this category.

Both types of expenses can get you into trouble. If your rent or mortgage costs you half a month's paycheck or more, that's a problem and you're living in a place that is causing you to go broke, *even if it is your dream house.* If you can barely make your auto payment, then you can't really afford the vehicle. Maybe a large chunk of your income is devoted to school loans, credit cards, or medical debt repayments. Not surprisingly, the same study from above that talked about 78% of workers living paycheck to paycheck also stated that 71% of those same individuals say they're in debt of some kind.

The question is: Do you want to keep living this way? Do you believe that you have a choice? Sometimes we get stuck in a belief pattern that leads us to believe we're destined to be in debt forever or that we'll never be able to break free from the paycheck-to-paycheck way of living, so we might as well accept it and just live life the best we can. If that's you, I applaud you for trying to put a positive spin on a very sad belief, but let's not give up hope yet! Let's take a look at what might be keeping you stuck.

There are a variety of reasons for why you might be living paycheck to paycheck and struggling to maintain a positive monthly cash flow. You might not even be able to come up with the reason at first. You just know that by the end of the month, you are trying to figure out how to get that last bill paid so you don't get another late fee.

There are some common patterns that I have seen in working with people in my financial coaching practice. If I were to narrow it down to one, though, it would probably be a refusal to give up and let go. We want what we want and we don't want to give up or let go of things even if they are costing us money (or more importantly, our freedom). In my client meetings, I often hear something to the effect of, "There's no way I can give up [this brand-new car that I *just* bought, for example]." They are stuck in "*I need this in my life*" and don't want to let it go. Trust me, I get it. I still want some luxuries in my life too. I'm not saying you have to give up all your indulgences, and I'm not trying to make you feel guilty or ashamed if you think this describes you. But I do want you to think about it. You've probably already had something come to mind that you know you're holding on to, right? I thought so.

Some believe that the primary reason they are struggling financially and living paycheck to paycheck is that they are not making enough money. Makes sense, right? Is that what you're thinking about your situation too? You just need to bring in more money? Well, I hate to tell you this, but rarely is the primary issue an income problem. It is almost always a planning or spending one. Let's look at what I mean by this.

When Planning is the Problem

When you are unprepared for a crisis, potential loss of income, or retirement, the root of the problem is usually a lack of planning. For example, you didn't have enough money saved when your water heater broke, so you had to use a credit card to pay for the repair. Or you bought your first home and you got starry eyed and it ended up costing you twice as much as you were initially going to spend; now you are held hostage to your mortgage payments because you didn't plan for how much house you could truly afford.

Planning takes time and requires focusing on the future and thinking about the what-ifs. Think about your last major purchase. Did you plan ahead for how you were going to pay for it or did you just whip out the credit card or go for the installment plan and figure you would work out how to pay for it later? I talk with people all the time who didn't plan for how much it might cost to do something like take a family vacation, buy a car, replace a roof, or even get married. I used to do the same thing. The problem is that it can end up creating a lot of undue stress.

When you don't *plan* for upcoming expenses and save up the money for them, you will often end up paying more than you expected and have to use a credit card or take out a loan for payment. Do this too many times and it can lead to some serious debt. It's never too early or too late to start planning, so we'll talk more about to create a plan for these kinds of expenses later in the book.

There are some situations that you might not think of planning for but can happen anyway. I call them the what-if events. For example, what would you do if you or your spouse lost a job or became disabled and couldn't work? How many months would you be able to pay your bills and support your family? Or what would happen if you became divorced or widowed? Would you have the financial resources to manage on your own or would you be like a fish out of water because your spouse always took care of the financial matters? What if you wanted to take in an adult child or an aging parent to live with you? How long would you be able to manage the extra expenses if they couldn't afford to help you financially?

Life can throw you a curve ball at any time. You may have already experienced this and know exactly what I'm talking about. When you don't plan for the what-if possibilities, they can wreak havoc on your financial future as well as your physical and emotional health.

If you're living paycheck to paycheck because you've *already* failed to plan appropriately for some things and you have lingering account balances that are accumulating monthly interest fees, raise your hand. It's okay. Hang in there and keep reading. In Chapters 12 and 13, we'll look at strategies to get you out of this trap!

Sonya's Story

I had a client named Sonya who initially had a hard time understanding the importance of planning. When I met her, she had $18,000 in credit card debt and a $5,000 personal loan, in addition to a $35,000 car loan, a couple of school loans, and a mortgage. She told me the credit card debt was from various expenses, including a vacation that she had taken to Hawaii two years prior, several department store purchases over the last couple of years, and Christmas from the prior year which she admits she overspent on. The personal loan was with her bank for some home repairs.

As we talked more about the debt, I asked her how much of it she had actually planned for. She looked at me blankly and then said, "None of it." They were spur of the moment transactions and things that she wanted even though she didn't have the money up front to pay for them. The vacation was something she felt that she deserved after a break-up with her boyfriend. She didn't need a new car when she bought it, but her emotions got the best of her. The home repairs were not critical at the time, but she didn't want to wait.

It didn't take long for her to understand that if she had just had a little bit of patience and saved up for those expenses, she would not have incurred all of the debt that she was then overwhelmed by.

I helped Sonia create a plan to pay off her debt and then we worked on how to plan for future expenses without accumulating more. She recently sent me an email letting me know that she was taking a small vacation that she had planned for and would be paying cash for it. Bingo!

When Spending is the Problem

A spending problem means that you are spending money on too many wants or living beyond your means. It can also be that you just have too many expenses or too high of expenses. In chapter 9, I have dedicated a whole chapter dedicated to triggers that cause us to overspend. For now, let's consider just a couple of examples:

1. You don't have any money at the end of the month because you're mindlessly spending on extras like eating out, massages, clothes, vacations, a cell phone plan with the newest smart phone, cable, or other goods and services that makes you feel or look good. Is your favorite hobby shopping online or in some department store? All those little shopping trips can really add up, especially if you're shopping online where you just keep putting your credit card number in and don't think about how much you've spent . . . until you get your statement. Did you catch the word *mindlessly*? It means you're not really thinking about what and how much you are spending. And honestly, at the time, you might not even care – until the

emotional high wears off or you start seeing your checking account dwindling down to nothing again.

Let me ask you this question. Do you have *expectations* of what your life should look like? What kind of house you should be living in? What kind of car you should be driving? What kind of vacations you should be taking? What kind of job you should have? These expectations of what you want and think you deserve can cause you to buy bigger and better. They make you compare yourself to your family, friends and neighbors and lead you to believe that you need to look like you have more or better stuff than they do. You start feeling like you don't measure up, and it can affect your self-esteem.

Personally, I had to take a look at where my expectations were coming from when I started thinking of changing my money behaviors. I remember growing up and watching television shows of the rich and famous and being enamored by the cool cars, large houses, exotic vacations and lots of money. A part of me desired that. It's not bad to want and have these things – *if* you can afford them. Too often, our expectations of what we want and believe we should have send us into destructive spending behaviors.

2. You don't have any money at the end of the month because you have children to take care of. After all, they cost a lot of money! It starts with preparing for their arrival. You buy paint for the room, decorations, stuffed animals, crib, stroller, toys, baby clothes, diapers, food and formula. If you're lucky, you got a head start with a baby shower and family and friends who graciously provided some of those things for you. Then, that joyful day arrived and not long afterwards came the hospital bills. Then, for the next twenty-plus years, you continue to spend money on these amazing gifts from God, making sure they have everything they need (and even some of

what you never had). I mean, really, have you gone shopping for kids lately? Their clothes cost more than for an adult! And let's not forget about school supplies, tuition costs, activities, and medical care. If you haven't prepared (there's that word again) for the expense of birthing and raising children, it can throw a couple into a financial tailspin, and even more so for a single parent. Yes, you have to spend money on your children. Just remember, your children love *you*, not what you buy them (although they will be quick to tell you that you don't love them when you don't buy them what they want!). It's okay. Use it as a money teaching moment. They'll thank you for it later.

I want to share a story with you about a couple of friends of mine from college who are raising eight children . . . debt free, with only one parent working. I had to know what their secrets were because I know that most parents struggle with living paycheck to paycheck. Hopefully, it encourages you to know that it is possible to raise kids without breaking the bank if you plan well and spend wisely.

Eight Kids and Debt Free

Chris and Mindy were each raised by frugal parents who didn't spend a lot of money on material things. They were taught that giving was more important than receiving and that it was important to live on less than they earned. From the start of their marriage, they agreed to live by those two principles. It wasn't always easy, especially in the beginning when Chris was still trying to get through his veterinary residency. It became even more difficult after each child. During those first few years, they were living paycheck to paycheck trying to stretch every dollar they received. Giving to their home church was – and always has been – their first monthly expense, no matter what. They believe that is what has allowed them to always be able to pay their bills.

Creating a plan and living on a budget has provided them the structure to make smart decisions with their money. They recognize that much of what they do with their money is a choice. They pay cash for most things and don't worry about those things being name-brand or brand-new. They bought a house that they knew they could afford and pay off quickly. They save up for vacations and other expensive purchases instead of using credit cards. They recently went to Israel and are making plans and saving up to take the whole family to Korea.

How have they been able to do this with eight kids on one income? Mindy told me that she and Chris are not afraid to say no, to themselves or to their kids. Their motto is, "Just because we can doesn't mean we will." Wow! I think it's a mantra we all need to put into practice, myself included. Although they are in a financial position now to buy brand-name and brand-new things if they want to, they continue to live by the two principles that they were taught as children: Give first and live on less than you earn.

You may be thinking that it was easier for my friends because Chris brought in a good income as a veterinarian. That is true – but they have *eight* children to support on that one income. The point is that they had to work together, determine their priorities, and agree with how to use the money. Mindy told me that every time their income went up, decisions about how to spend their money became harder. There were internal conflicts in regards to what they wanted versus what they needed as a family. When their children asked why they couldn't have the latest video game or clothes that were the latest fashion trend, it was difficult to tell them no. But they did.

Spending is not inherently bad. It becomes a problem when you spend too much or spend on things you cannot afford. And it becomes an issue when it conflicts with your priorities and values. Go ahead and turn to chapter 9 if you can't wait to read more about the topic of spending in greater detail. Just make sure you come back and finish this chapter!

When Income is the Problem

When you're living paycheck to paycheck, it might feel like lack of income is the problem. If you just had more money coming in, things would be different, right? I hear my clients say that all the time. And it may be true . . . at least for the time being. Let's consider three possible situations that you may be in.

First, you don't bring in much money. You might earn minimum wage or live off of disability or social security income. Or your income might be okay if you were single but not for your family of four. Or you may live in an area that has a higher cost of living, so the money that you do make doesn't go as far compared to an area with a lower cost of living.

Second, your income used to be enough to provide for your needs but expenses have increased and now it's not enough. You're already working more than one job and have cut your expenses to the bare necessities. Yet you still struggle to bring in the income you need to get ahead and become financially stable.

Lastly, you bring in a really good income; it may even be a great income. You don't have a lot of debt accumulated aside from your house and school loans, but you still find yourself not having much money left over at the end of each month to build your savings or plan for upcoming expenses.

If you're facing a lack of income problem for whatever reason, you may feel physically, mentally, and emotionally exhausted. Your mind may be in a constant mode of trying to figure out how to spend less or how to bring in extra money. You may be fighting with your spouse or find yourself getting easily frustrated with your children and others around you because you're so tired. I get it.

The thing about the income problem is that it usually isn't about how much money you make. More often than not, the problem goes back to lack of planning and overspending, which you read about earlier in this chapter. Could this be true for you? It was for me.

Let me ask you a few questions. What decisions have you made that might have contributed to your current financial situation? Looking back, did you buy things that you couldn't really afford? Did you neglect to plan effectively for a big event? Did a what-if crisis throw you off track because you didn't have any money saved up to deal with it?

The bigger issue is that most of us try to live *beyond* our paycheck. And if you live beyond your paycheck for too many months, it will eventually become an income problem. Now . . . I'm not saying that the financial situation you find yourself in is all your fault and you should have known better. I simply want us to look at the bigger picture to determine what the problem really is.

I know that trying to support yourself or your family on minimum wage is definitely going to be more of a challenge than if you are making two or three times that. If income has become the problem because it is no longer enough to pay all your monthly expenses and is keeping you in the paycheck-to-paycheck trap, then you have some decisions to make. Here are a few to consider:

- Do you look for a different job or find a different career that will pay you more money? This might mean moving from the nonprofit sector to for profit.
- Do you give up your stagnant business or "passion" career to go back into the traditional workforce?
- Do you look for a second job to supplement what you're already making?
- Does the stay-at-home spouse need to get a job?
- Do you downsize your car or move into a less expensive house?
- Do you move to a city that has a lower cost of living?
- Do you need to get some assistance from an agency for a while to help you get back on your feet?

Having to consider one of these changes is tough. It can be difficult to think about giving up the dream job that you are in even though you aren't making enough money from it. It's hard to think about the possibility of moving or asking for help. But if it frees you from the stress and exhaustion you're experiencing, is it worth it?

I've worked with families that made well over six figures. Yet, they were living paycheck to paycheck. How can that be? Well, they kept spending all the money that they brought in. *If you don't know how to manage your money and control your behaviors, you will end up wondering where it went at the end of every month regardless of how much income you bring in.*

Even people with low-paying jobs can retire with wealth. I've heard and read many stories of people who had normal everyday jobs who retired comfortably. How do they do it? They all tend to have the same secret, which is planning ahead for their expenses and living way below their income. They made conscious choices about how to manage their money.

What is Keeping You Stuck?

So, what is keeping you stuck living paycheck to paycheck or unable to give, save, or invest as you would like to? It's probably not just one specific thing but a combination. When I was living this lifestyle, I loved to shop and spent way too much money on clothes, house décor, and other wants. But I also went on vacations that I couldn't afford. I went out to eat a lot because I didn't like to cook. I lived in apartments that cost too much and then I bought a house that almost made me broke because I didn't realize how much it was going to cost to furnish and decorate it. I had a planning problem *and* a spending problem! It was about my *behaviors*, not the amount of money coming in.

We tend to underestimate the number of other families that are living paycheck to paycheck. We make assumptions about our family, friends, neighbors, and coworkers based on what we see and hear. We assume that they can afford the things they have bought (just as they assume you can afford the things you have bought). Do you ever feel like everyone around you seems to be enjoying life while you're stressing out about how to pay for the dentist bill that you got last week? We do a really good job of putting on a mask that leads others to believe we're doing great financially.

The great news is that you can change your situation!

You don't have to continue living paycheck to paycheck. I want you to be able to provide abundantly for your family, give generously, and save sufficiently. I'm not going to say it will be easy. It's going to take different choices, habits, and mindsets. Decide today that you're tired of not having enough money at the end of each month and are ready to change. Make a commitment to finish this book, do the activities, and pray for direction.

Don't panic! I can already sense you tensing up and getting anxious. I promise that I'm not going to tell you that you have to live a minimalist lifestyle (unless that appeals to you, then go for it) or that you have to give up everything and not have any more fun. Stay with me and keep learning from others who have been where you are. When I decided that I was ready for a change in my financial situation, it was reading stories of how others succeeded that gave me hope and kept me moving forward.

NOTE: You might already be thinking, "Tina, you don't understand. *I didn't get into this situation because of bad decisions on my part.*" "I went through a painful divorce and was left with nothing." "My family has had one medical crisis after another which insurance has not been able to cover." "My spouse died and didn't have a life insurance policy, and he/she was the sole financial provider." I do understand, and I want you to keep reading because the same principles can apply for you. You can't change what has happened, but you *can* fight for a different future.

In the next few chapters, you will discover how your experiences around money have influenced how you manage money. As a counselor, I like looking at the past and how it has affected our current self. As a coach, I help people focus on the present and move forward without spending too much time on the past. In this book, you will encounter both sides of the coin so to speak in regard to you and your money. First, you are going to learn about your *money story* and your *money mindset*. We will talk about them in depth next.

Spiritual Perspective

I do not believe God's plan and desire is for us to lead a paycheck-to-paycheck lifestyle in which we are constantly stressed about money and feeling like we cannot provide for our families. I think He wants us to live and give abundantly. That doesn't mean we are all meant to be millionaires and that God is going to make us all wealthy. It does mean that He will provide for us financially, and it's our responsibility to faithfully and efficiently manage whatever He gives us. Unfortunately, most of us don't do a very good job with that last part.

You may be familiar with the Bible verse, "It is easier for a camel to go through the eye of a needle than for someone who is rich to enter the Kingdom of God" (Mark 10:25), and the story about the poor widow in Mark 12:41-44 who was praised by Jesus because she gave all she had to live on. I grew up believing that it was best not to have too much money, as these verses seem to endorse. I walked that line between wanting to have a lot of money and believing it was wrong.

As I got older, though, I realized that I missed the context surrounding those passages. Having money is not bad. There were actually a lot of devoted believers in the Bible who were very wealthy and still blessed by God. But having more money means more responsibility in managing it. When we overspend and take on a lot of debt, we are not managing money wisely.

Even people in ministry, including our pastors and missionaries should be able to make enough money to live comfortably. Why is it that so many of us Christians believe that our pastors should not live in a nice house or drive a nice car? I remember when I found out that a pastor I knew lived in an expensive home in a much nicer neighborhood than I did. I questioned that pastor's integrity and use of money. Looking back, I realize how wrong it was for me to think that way. It is not for me to judge anyone else for what they have been blessed with. Had I managed my money more wisely, I could have lived in that same area!

Are you walking around with a mask on? Do you go to church or Bible Study pretending like everything is okay or comparing yourself with the other members? I find that people in church often struggle to be honest about their financial situation, with themselves and with others. Maybe it's because we think we have to project an image that says everything is okay. Maybe it's because we're embarrassed for people in the church to know how much we've messed up.

It's time to stop hiding and start dealing with your situation. God wants to bless you abundantly. But, as the saying goes, why would He give you more when you cannot handle what you currently have? Hmmm . . .

Planning Your Escape

1. Make a list of what you think is keeping you living paycheck to paycheck or keeps you from not having enough money at the end of each month.

2. Are you willing to consider making some changes to your habits, behaviors, or attitude around money so you can start moving forward?

   _______ Yes _______ No _______ I'm not sure yet

3. What is your biggest takeaway from Chapter 2?

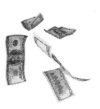

CHAPTER 3

Money Stories and Money Mindsets

Have you ever thought about how people (parents, grandparents, teachers, neighbors, pastors, and Sunday school teachers) and experiences from your childhood have influenced the way you live your life today? Who was your favorite teacher in school? Why? What was the best piece of advice that you still remember today? What negative experience impacted you the most? Did your parents get divorced? Did you get cut from the sports team that you so desperately wanted to be part of? Were you told that you weren't good enough? Did you strive to get all A's because you got in trouble at home if you didn't? Did you win an award for a special achievement?

We all had these kinds of moments growing up, times that brought us joy and others that brought us to our knees in tears. Some have made lasting impressions on how we think, behave and interact today. They are stories that we carry around with us in our subconscious minds. For example, if your parents divorced when you were young, you may have trust issues in your relationships because you fear that you will be hurt again by getting too close and then having that person walk away. If you didn't make the basketball team or cheerleading squad in high school, you may have learned that it is better to just sit on the sidelines than to actively participate because you would just embarrass yourself.

Now think about how individuals and different experiences you had when growing up have influenced how you view and interact with *money*. What did you learn about money from your parents? Let's look at a few quick examples. Holly learned that it was important to save for a rainy day and put that money in a really safe place at home where no one would think to look for it. Jack remembers being told that he needed to be a doctor or lawyer if he wanted to make enough money to take care of a family when he got older. Sandy said her parents fought about money all the time, and she feared they would get a divorce and she would be out on the street and unable to go to school. These memories are what coaches and counselors often call pieces of your "money story" which is a collection of the thoughts, feelings, lessons, and beliefs you have learned from influential people in your life and experiences you have had. It begins in childhood and builds and transforms through adulthood. I encourage my clients to look at their money story because it creates a new awareness about why they might be struggling with money issues.

Your money story can help you make sense of why you might have made or continue to make some of the decisions that you do. It can help you understand why you might be more of a spender instead of a saver or vice versa or why you tend to underearn. For example, if you grew up in a household where there was rarely enough money for you to have a new pair of jeans or shoes, then you might have what is called a scarcity mentality and have a tendency to overspend so you can finally have whatever you want. On the other hand, you might become an extreme saver so you never have to worry about your survival again.

When you share your story with your partner or spouse, it helps expose why you two are on the same page or constantly at odds over how to handle money. You may marry someone who either thinks similar to you about money or is your polar opposite. Either one can get you trouble. How? If you are both spenders, it will be difficult to save for pretty much anything. If you're both savers, you might have a hard time seeing why spending money to go on a vacation to Disney World is attractive to other families. If one is a saver and one is a spender, there will be friction in the relationship if you're not communicating and understanding where the other person is coming from. It's important to understand that what you saw, heard and experienced growing up has had more influence than you know on how you deal with and relate to your money and also how you relate with the people around you.

Similarly, your money mindset is an attitude or set of opinions that you have about money. Those early experiences, thoughts, teachings and mistakes about money are what help create that mindset. Here are some common phrases about money that you may have heard and adopted as true:

- Money doesn't grow on trees (meaning it's not easy to get or infinitely available).
- Money is the root of all evil (actually, the correct phrase from the Bible is "the *love* of money is the root of all evil," not money itself).
- Having a lot of money is selfish.
- Credit cards are (a) evil pieces of plastic you need to stay away from or (b) a great way to receive more money through rewards points.
- Keep your savings safely at home because you can't trust the banks with it; and if there is a world crisis, you might not be able to get your money out.
- Those who have little are held in higher esteem by God and the church than those who have much.
- You need to save for a rainy day.

If you heard any of these phrases over and over again as a kid, you can see how it would have an impact on how you view money as an adult. Think about this for a minute. Do you spend or give all your money away because you were told it was "bad" to have too much? Do you hoard your money because you grew up in scarcity and are afraid you'll never have enough? Are you a woman afraid to talk about money with your spouse because you learned that taking care of financial matters is the "husband's responsibility"? These thoughts and feelings can inhibit you from having a healthy relationship with money and in turn deter you from financial success. It can keep you living paycheck to paycheck!

So, let's look at this area a little more in depth. Over the next three chapters, you will explore three periods in your life when your money story and mindset would have been shaped. As I ask you to start thinking about *your* money story and mindset, I will be sharing some of mine. We'll start with the earliest memories that have helped shape us. As you will see from mine, even some of those experiences that seemed insignificant at the time, have stuck with me and taught me something about money and made an impact on my mindset. Quite likely, the same is true for you.

If you are a parent, this is also a great time to think about your children and the fact that they are creating their money story right now! What do you want them to know and experience about money before they become adults?

Spiritual Perspective

Your money story has also been shaped by the influential people and experiences that you had in church, youth group, or other religious organizations. Was the role of money discussed in your church or among the members? What kinds of sermons did the pastor give around money; what were the messages about? I've heard a lot of people say that the only thing they remember is their pastor preaching about tithing and always trying to get them to give more money to the church. If that's all you heard, you may have developed a negative association with church and money.

What Bible stories did you hear or read that included messages about money? What lessons did you learn about money through these stories? Is it better to be rich or poor? Or does it matter in the eyes of God?

Spend some time thinking about what you've learned about money and how it relates to your walk with God as you read the next couple of chapters. It's our responsibility to manage money in a way that honors and glorifies Him. But what is that way? I hope you will have clarity on this by the time you finish reading this book.

Planning Your Escape

- What are some things that you learned or experienced growing up that you think might have contributed to your money story or your beliefs around money? Just pick two or three that come to mind right away.

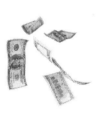

CHAPTER 4

The Early Years

When I was growing up in La Porte, Indiana, my parents didn't have a lot of money. They definitely lived paycheck to paycheck. My dad was a police officer and my mom stayed at home with me and my younger brother. We lived in a small three-bedroom, one-bathroom ranch house that my parents rented from another couple down the street. It was a nice little neighborhood with good families and a lot of kids. We had a great yard and a quiet street that allowed us to play games like kick the can and freeze tag (remember those?).

Having a family of four on an officer's salary was tough on my parents. But I don't remember hearing them fight about money. In fact, I don't really remember any conversations about money when I was a kid. There was always food on the table and favorite toys for birthdays and Christmases. We were able to take annual family vacations to visit my paternal grandparents in Florida and my maternal grandparents in North Dakota. My parents did a nice job of shielding us from the stress of their paycheck-to-paycheck lifestyle, so the early memories of my money story are pretty positive. It wouldn't be until many years later, that I would find out how tough it was on my parents to provide those gifts and experiences for us.

Your money story is about looking at both the positive and negative words, behaviors, and experiences that you've encountered throughout your life so far. It's incorporating everything that you've seen, heard, and learned. As you walk down memory lane, you will find that there are some experiences that helped shape your money story more than others. Some of them might seem trivial, but you want to look at the whole picture when constructing your story. Usually, the things that we remember vividly are what have made a unique impact on our lives. See if you can relate to any of mine. You will notice that after the memory, I have included its impact.

As a young child, I remember:

- Getting a quarter from the tooth fairy every time I lost a baby tooth. Oh, the excitement of waking up that next morning and reaching under my pillow to see my tooth replaced with a shiny object instead! I think this is one of my first memories of getting free money, although there was some pain involved when a tooth didn't want to come out!
- Running a Kool-Aid stand in my neighborhood once or twice. That was my first toe dip into the exciting world of entrepreneurship. Never would I have thought that one day I would actually be running my own business.
- When I started to get money instead of (or in addition to)

gifts for birthdays and Christmas. Although I loved unwrapping presents, there was something to be said for seeing and feeling dollar bills in my hand and then being able to buy something that I wanted with my own money.

- My parents letting me put their money into the offering plate at church. I didn't really understand the importance at the time, but it was my first introduction to giving and tithing (giving a portion of your earned money to your place of worship).
- Having a piggy bank to save up for things. I loved to hear the jingle of coins and feel it get heavier as more coins were added, and then I really loved counting the coins to see how much money I had saved. (Too bad I also really loved spending that money!)

What I remember most, though, is my dad working more than one job at a time. Being a police officer was his full-time job, but he also had various part-time jobs, including working at a motorcycle shop, auto dealership, and a transportation center. This did come in handy for me one year when I had set a goal to sell the most Girl Scout cookies in our unit. My dad took me to all of his past and current jobs and introduced me to all of his coworkers. I sold boxes and boxes of cookies! And yes, I was the top seller that year thanks to my dad.

What I learned from my dad that is a big part of my money story and mindset was that you need to have more than one job in order to make ends meet and keep food on the table for your family. One job alone is not enough. It shouldn't surprise you to know, then, that as an adult I have almost always had more than one job at a time.

I've always felt like I needed to earn *more*. I know that is not what he would have wanted me to learn from him about money, but it is the one thing that has always stood out to me in my early childhood memory.

Your experiences may be very different. You may have memories of your parents fighting about money and maybe even divorcing because of it. Or maybe you remember too many times when there was no food on the table, or you had to wear the same clothes to school every day because there was no money to buy you anything and other kids made fun of you. Maybe you grew up in a household with maids and nannies and vacations to exotic locations, but you never got to spend time with your parents. When you were young, did you live on the "poor" side of town, the "rich" side of town, or somewhere in between? Looking back, did that influence how you thought about yourself or others? Did adults ever say things that led you to believe you were good or bad because of how much or how little your family had?

Kids pay attention to what is going on around them. Whether you have children of your own, have nieces and nephews, or spend time with neighbors' or friends' kids, I'm sure you've noticed they're like sponges absorbing everything we say and do and often asking a dozen questions about it. You were probably the same way when you were young. That's why I'm asking a lot of questions here to jog your memory about things around your experiences related to money. Often, we don't even know how those things will shape our lives as adults. It wasn't until I got older that I realized the impact of watching my dad constantly have more than one job or the sacrifices my parents made so my brother and I could have our favorite toys.

So, here are a couple more questions to think about in regards to cold hard cash. You remember what dollar bills and coins look like, right? I know it's becoming a bit of an anomaly to have cash when debit cards, credit cards and online payments are the more acceptable forms of payment. But, let's talk about it for a minute anyway.

Do you remember the first time you received a dollar bill or a five-dollar bill or better yet, a twenty? How old were you? Do you remember the thoughts and feelings surrounding that experience? There is something to be said for actually handling cash (even if it's fake cash like when playing Monopoly). It can make you feel powerful and important. You can actually get emotionally connected to it. I love the feel of cash. I love counting cash. And yes, sometimes I really love spending it. For the longest time, I thought that it seemed like such a waste for money to just sit in my piggy bank (or my savings account when I got older). Nowadays, I have a much harder time parting with it and watching it easily slip through my fingers. Now, I actually enjoy keeping it in a savings or investment account and watching it grow!

Hopefully, these questions and examples have brought up some memories for you that you connect with.

Whether positive or negative, we all have experiences from our early childhood that have influenced how we view and what we do with money today. That first piggy bank might have been the catalyst that encouraged you to always save. Parents fighting about money or Dad saying "No, we can't afford that" might have led you to believe that you were on the verge of losing everything. Just because you were young doesn't mean you weren't watching, listening, and feeling.

But, here's another thing to consider – something that may have seemed like a painful or embarrassing experience when you were young may have actually taught you a valuable lesson. Watching your parent buy a toy for a child in need but not buy you something that you wanted may have taught you about generosity and putting others first. Growing up without a lot of money may have taught you how to live and appreciate a more simplified life and learn ways to live within your means. You may have also learned that family is much more important than how much money you have.

It's all about perspective, being aware of your story and embracing it. You can choose to focus on the negative things that you saw, heard, or felt. Or you can figure out how to turn it into a positive.

If you have children or grandchildren, they are doing the same thing – watching, listening, and experiencing various emotions. They are listening to what you say about money and watching how you spend it. You have a pivotal role in helping to develop their money story and money mindset. I don't say this to scare you and make you think that you are going to traumatize your kids and give them a bad money story. I say it to encourage you to be aware of your own story and then open the lines of communication with them. Take some time to think about what you want them to know about money at this early age.

One of the things you can do is give your kids three jars or envelopes labeled giving, saving, and spending. It might be more fun if you let them decorate and label the jars or labels themselves. Teach them that when they receive money for things like birthdays, Christmas, or an allowance, they need to put a percentage into each one. You might tell them to put 10% into the giving jar, 10% into the savings jar and 80% into the spending jar. This will help them learn at a young age that there is more to do with money than just spend it. You will also want to share with them why the giving and savings jars are important so they understand why they need to put money in them.

Spiritual Perspective

It's our responsibility as Christian parents, family members and influential people in a child's life to teach them about managing money God's way (and probably to show them how to do it better than we've done it so far). They are counting on us to help create a positive money story and mindset for them. You cannot do this if you haven't come to terms with your own story or learned to manage your own money in a healthy, God-honoring way. No one is saying you have to do this perfectly (which is impossible, by the way). It's okay to make mistakes, we all do. In fact, it's in failing and making mistakes that we *all* learn.

I think one of the most important things you can do is to teach your kids and grandkids early about giving and tithing. I know that if you are living paycheck to paycheck you may not a have a lot to give. That's okay. It's just important for your kids to see you giving *something* to the church even if it's only a dollar. And let them put something in the plate as it goes by. If you give them an allowance, I encourage you to tell them they must put a percentage of their allowance into the offering plate, maybe 5%-10% (so, if you give them one dollar every week, they should put five or ten cents of it in the offering plate every week). I strongly encourage you to explain why giving is important and why you do it. It makes it a little easier to part with that "hard-earned" cash when you know why.

Note: If you're not giving money to your church or a favorite charity, then don't expect your kids to value this concept. Be careful about telling them to do something that you're not willing to do yourself!

Planning Your Escape

1. Now, it's your turn. Brainstorm and record your *earliest* memories about money using the examples in this chapter as guidelines. (Think up to age eleven or twelve). Be as specific as possible and list as many things as you can think of. Remember, this is early childhood. We'll get into your teen years in the next chapter.

2. How might these childhood memories have impacted how you interact with money today? What lessons did you learn?

3. What do you want to teach your young children and grandchildren about money? What do you want them to know?

4. What activities can you do with them to help them understand how to manage money?

5. Make a point to talk with your kids about money and talk with them early. Let them know that it's okay to ask questions if they don't understand something and then be as honest as you can with them about the answers.

CHAPTER 5

The Impressionable Years

The years between ages twelve and eighteen are some of the most impressionable – even when it comes to your money story and mindset. The experiences you had during these years can have a profound effect on how you view and deal with money as an adult. Let's look at a couple of snapshot stories to get a better idea of what I mean by this.

Sheila and Gary

At sixteen, Sheila remembers, she had to take care of her two younger siblings while her single mom worked two jobs. She would get up each morning to make them breakfast and get them ready for school. After school, she would help them with their homework, make dinner, and get them ready for bed. Sheila resented that she had to be the parent to her brother and sister and didn't understand why her mom was always working. While her friends were going to parties and movies, she was home babysitting. While her friends were working and getting paid, she was expected to babysit for free. Sheila ended up starting her own business when she was an adult, but her experiences as a teenager left her stuck in a negative mindset of not being worthy enough to be paid for her value, so she constantly struggled to meet her financial goals.

Gary, on the other hand, had a very different experience in his teen years. His parents did very well financially and were able to lavish him and his brother with lots of things. They even bought him a brand-new expensive car when he was sixteen. He didn't have to worry about having to pay for anything because his parents always gave him whatever he wanted. Not surprisingly, when he finally started working after college, he spent all of his money on "stuff" because that was what he was accustomed to. It didn't take long, however, for Gary to find himself broke and seeking money from his parents to help pay off a bunch of debt that he had accumulated.

These impressionable years are also a time when you might have really started looking at what others had that you didn't, or what you had that others didn't. The middle school and high school years are often about fitting in and keeping up. Think back to your formative years. Who was wearing the latest fashion trends? Who seemed to always be going on vacation with their family? Who lived in a big, two-story house? Who always had money to go out to eat or to the movies or the club? Was it you? Or was it your peers?

You also listened to the conversations going on around you a little more intently. You watched the people closest to you and the decisions they made with a different set of eyes. During this stage you started being even more aware of what your parents spent their money on. Which of these experiences did you most identify with as a teenager?

- Your parents graciously gave you mostly everything you wanted, like paying for piano or swimming lessons, summer camps, or your favorite brand of jeans or shoes without complaining about the expense.
- Your parents spent money more on themselves. They always told you there wasn't enough money to buy you what you wanted but then you would see them come home with something new for themselves.
- Your parent was a saver and didn't think money should be spent on anything other than necessities. You would get one or two small gifts for Christmas while your friends were getting three or four.
- Your parent became sick or disabled and was unable to work or lost their job. As a result, you remember your family having to give up many of the luxuries they had grown accustomed to.
- Your parent squandered money on addictive behaviors like alcohol, cigarettes, or gambling. How many times did they put their need for this addiction in front of your needs and wants?

- Your parents played favorites with you and your siblings. Were you the favored child who got everything you wanted or the one feeling bitter and jealous because you couldn't even get a new pair of shoes? How did this impact your relationships with your parents and your siblings?
- Your parent worked tirelessly just to make sure you had food and clothes. Maybe you grew up with a single parent who had to work two or more jobs. Did you resent it or appreciate it?
- Your family never seemed to have enough money to even pay the utilities, and your parents were always fighting. You lived in fear that the electricity would be turned off or that you would get kicked out of your home.

Can you see how these experiences might have influenced how you relate to and manage money as an adult? Those feelings of protection or fear, security or insecurity, love or betrayal – they helped shape your money story. Chances are good that you experienced more than just one of these scenarios, because our lives are not stagnant. Things change. Events happen that can throw a perfectly secure situation out of balance, like a parent becoming chronically ill or losing a job, which results in loss of income.

If your experiences are mostly negative or fear-based, you'll probably need to do some soul searching and try to find some good in them. We'll talk about this more in Chapter 7 where I will give you some tips on how to change your story and your mindset. But hold on, don't go there yet.

During this time of impressionable years, you also started forming prejudices and opinions based on your experiences and what your family and friends led you to believe. Again, these helped shape your *mindset* which Webster's describes as a "fixed mental attitude." Remember, your parents, grandparents, neighbors, and teachers also had their own money stories, which they internalized and in turn felt obligated to share with you. Those mindset stories can then become your stories as well. Here are some mindset statements that you might have heard growing up:

- "Success means having a lot of money."
- "You'll never make a living doing *that*."
- "Minority people are poor."
- "Rich people are arrogant and selfish."
- "You have to work really hard to be successful and make it financially."
- "It is not good to have a lot of money. You should give it to those less fortunate."
- "It is better to be poor than to be rich."
- "If at first you don't succeed, keep trying and never give up."

Hearing these types of comments over and over at an impressionable age can certainly impact how you view those around you as well as how you view yourself. If you grew up being told that rich people are arrogant and selfish and it is better to be poor, chances are you are not rich. Your money mindset tells you that having money is bad. If you watched your parents work an excessive number of hours and they told you that you have to work hard in order to be successful and have money, you probably tend to spend more time at your job than at home with your family because you need to show them how hard you are working for them.

You may also have heard about how certain careers can make you rich and others can keep you poor. When you were a teenager trying to decide what to major in during college, what led you in that direction? Was it how much money you could make? When you told people that you wanted to be a social worker, writer, artist, comedian, or actor, did people tell you that you would starve because you would never make any money? Did they have a different career in mind for you? How did that influence your decision?

Did you squash your dreams to do what was expected of you and fulfill someone else's dreams for your future? If so, you're not alone. Many people I have talked with gave up a dream so that they could be what someone else wanted them to be. They became a doctor instead of a firefighter, a lawyer instead of an artist, or a partner in the family business instead of a teacher. Sometimes it works out, but often when you follow someone else's dream, you end up feeling unhappy and cheated. You reach your forties and realize that you really don't like your life or your job and you feel stuck. You might even look for ways to change it . . . if it's not too late. Do you know someone who finally is doing what they dreamed about as a child, but it came as a second career or during retirement? It's never too late.

Let's look at an example of how prejudice can affect our mindset.

When I was growing up, the only homeless people I remember seeing were on television. My understanding was that they were homeless because they didn't have any family or any money. They lived on the streets, pushed carts with their belongings, wore dirty clothes, and ate out of dumpsters or hung out on street corners begging for food. They were normally grumpy and somewhere I got the idea that they were mentally ill. This was my mindset about this particular group of people based on limited messages I received as a child and teenager. I bring up this population as an example because many fear becoming homeless at some level.

When you see a homeless person, what goes through your mind? What kinds of assumptions do you make? Do you feel sorry for them and wonder what has happened in their life to bring them to that point? Or do you believe they are con artists and that they just need to go find a job? Does it instill fear in you because it makes you think how easily you could end up in their position? Why do you respond that way? What experience have you had or what have you heard that leads you to your first reaction? How does it confirm or conflict with what you learned about this group of people in general?

I will admit that I used to have a negative reaction when I would see someone living on the streets or standing on a street corner with a sign asking for food or a job. I never understood what would put someone in that situation. Even when I was in a lot of debt, I'm not sure I imagined myself actually being homeless. So, that must be their *choice*. I figured they must be lazy or trying to trick people into giving them money – until I talked with a couple of them and heard their stories. The ones I spoke with were down on their luck and embarrassed about their situation. One was a young man who had lost his job and struggled to find a new one. Without a job he was unable to afford rent, so he lost his apartment and was living in his car. Things spiraled out of control and he just couldn't get back on his feet again.

It was wrong of me to assume that all homeless people have the same story, but my assumption at the time was based on my mindset of what I thought or knew to be true at the time. Had I not stepped outside of my comfort zone to have a conversation, I would still be stuck in my negative mindset and overgeneralizing that population.

What if it's not a person on the street corner but the disheveled person you see sitting across from you at your child's school event or next to you in church? Does that make a difference in how you see and respond to them? Do you look at them with embarrassment or shame, or do you have a higher tolerance for them? Sometimes, it's difficult to be around people who don't "look like" us, even in a shared space.

Now, think about the opposite end of the spectrum. What is your initial reaction when you find out a coworker drives an expensive car and lives in a much wealthier neighborhood than you? Do you look at that person differently than when you thought they were in the same kind of financial situation as you? Do you wonder how they were able to afford it? Do you judge them for what they're driving and where they live? What does your money story tell you about wealthy people and therefore this coworker?

What do you think when a friend or family member has just told you that they are planning to declare bankruptcy? You know that they have spent a lot of money on their house, going on vacations, and so forth. You assumed that they were doing really well financially, even better than you. Do you judge? Do you feel tricked? What experience from your past leads you to feel these things? How does it affect your relationship with them?

What prejudices do you have around money and gender, culture, race, and religion? Should men make more money than women? In your mind, is a certain culture or group of people better with money? Who do you believe is more giving? Who is more selfish?

I know . . . that was *a lot* of questions! Here's the thing. Despite what we see, hear, or think we know about the people around us, reality is often much different. That coworker in the expensive house may actually be in major debt but refuses to give up the house because of what it would look like to her family and friends. The disheveled person sitting next to you in church may actually have thousands of dollars sitting in a bank account but is embarrassed or doesn't feel worthy of having that much money, so they don't let anyone know. *Their* mindsets and money stories are having a profound impact on their lives as well.

Are *you* the one that others are making assumptions about? Do you drive around in an old beat-up car when you could actually afford a fancy new car? Maybe you could even pay cash for it without it making a dent in your bank account? Do you drive an older car because a new car isn't of value to you, or is it because you don't think you deserve it or you fear spending that much money? On the other hand, maybe you live in an impressive house that others are jealous of. But, it also came with a hefty new mortgage (because you didn't have enough money for a decent down payment), and you already have a mountain of debt. What prompted the purchase? Desire to fit in? Attention? Oh, I know . . . it was your spouse's idea, right? It's time to start getting honest with yourself. Not to lay blame, shame, or guilt on anyone – including yourself – but to recognize why you make some of the choices that you do.

Can you see how understanding what you learned from those closest to you about money and the people who have it or don't have it has shaped your story? In the next chapter, we are going to finish by looking at how experiences in your adult years have changed or solidified your story.

Spiritual Perspective

As a teenager, what messages did you get from your parents and church family about God and money? You may have received a subtle message, like having to dress really nicely in dresses and suits or people would look at you in disgust and shake their head. Do you remember hearing, "Put on your Sunday best" or being told that dressing up was a sign of respect when you enter God's house? I do. Sometimes, it still doesn't feel right to wear jeans or shorts to church. I had to get past the idea that it's not about what we wear but the attitude of our heart. I don't need to go out and buy new clothes to look good at church, and neither do you.

I grew up reading and hearing Bible stories such as the widow who was recognized and praised by Jesus for giving all she had out of her poverty, the disciples who gave up everything they had to follow Jesus, and the rich man having a harder time getting into heaven. These stories led me to believe that I wouldn't be a good "Christian" if I had too much money. I thought that it was more noble to be a missionary or pastor and not have a lot of money. I was often uncomfortable being around wealthy people. When I got older, I realized that those Bible stories were often taken out of context and were teaching tools that Jesus used to help us understand discipline, integrity, and what it means to follow Him. I also started to see that there were all kinds of people in the Bible that were blessed by God regardless of their career or how much or how little money they had.

I had to be open to a different way of thinking about what I had learned about God and money as a teenager. You might need to do that as well. Is what you learned from your parents and church family serving you well or keeping you stuck?

____

Planning Your Escape

1. Take a moment to write what you remember about your parents and other influential adults regarding how they used money and what they taught you about money during your predominantly teen years.

2. What money mindset phrases did you hear when you were growing up that have stuck with you?

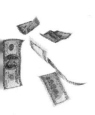

3. What did you learn from the following people and institutions about money when you were a teenager? Who made the most significant impact on your life, whether it was positive or negative? Review the following list and put a star by that person.

   Mom:

   Dad:

   Grandparents:

   Church:

   Teacher:

   Other Family Member:

   Neighbor:

   Friends:

   Youth Leader:

CHAPTER 6

The Adult Years

Your money story and money mindset beliefs do not end when you turn eighteen or twenty-one years old. They continue to evolve as you have more experiences and meet new people with different stories and mindsets, which can influence you in a positive or negative way. Luckily, you can change your story and mindset once you become aware of what they are and how they are impacting your life. Karla is one of my former clients who did this when she realized how her son was going to be impacted by the money decisions she and her husband were making.

Karla's story

Karla grew up in a typical middle-class family where her parents made good money but still lived paycheck to paycheck. She and her sister were both involved in school activities. Karla played basketball and her sister was a track star. They took annual vacations to fun places and because of their busy lifestyle, the family often went out to eat. She heard her parents argue about money, but she didn't realize how bad things were until they sat her down during her senior year in high school and told her that they didn't have any money to send her to her top college choice. Karla was devastated.

Fast forward: At age thirty-four, married with a child of her own, Karla saw herself making the same mistakes as her parents, earning a good income but spending more money than they brought in and accumulating a lot of debt. She didn't want to have to tell her son that she didn't have money for him to attend college like her parents told her. So, she and her husband made some tough decisions that included bringing in some extra money, spending less, and increasing savings. They might not have enough for him to attend a private school, but at least they would be able to help him afford a good public state college. She used her past money story – and her mindset about living large without worrying about the future – to change her present one and that of her child's. THAT is changing a legacy!

In your childhood and teen years, your money story and mindset develop mostly by what you see, hear, and experience from those closest to you. As an adult, *you* are primarily responsible for their evolvement. People and situations may still influence you, but you get to decide how. Here are some examples that can affect your money story and mindset during your adult years:

- You keep getting yourself into a lot of debt and determine that you will never be good with money; there must be something wrong with you.

- You love to spend money, so you figure that you will need to keep working forever; no retiring for you!
- You make a bad investment decision and get burned or lose a bunch of money in a stock market crash, which leads you to not want to invest in anything ever again.
- You run your own business but constantly undercharge because you feel bad charging more and don't value what you're actually worth, so you never make a decent profit
- You visit a family or group of families that are considered very poor and yet they have smiles on their faces and love in their hearts; you are led to re-examine your thoughts and feelings about what you have and don't have as well as your priorities about "stuff" in general.
- You were brought up to be a saver and you've always been good at saving your money. Then, you met your spouse, who is a spender. You got caught up in the thrill of spending money and now your savings is depleted and you can't figure out how to get back to where you were.
- You learn that a charity you had given a lot of money to just got in trouble for mismanaging its money; now you are suspicious of giving to any other charities or organizations and decide to just save the money for yourself.
- Someone from a different race or culture than you gets the promotion that you were hoping for, so you make a general assumption that they were given the promotion to balance out potential discrimination. You decide you'll never get a promotion, so why even try.

These are just a few possible examples. Maybe you can relate with one or two of them. Consider what other experiences you have had as an adult that have changed the way you deal with money, either in a positive or a negative way.

Fear-Based Money Mindsets

Now let's talk about a couple of specific money mindsets that seem to have pervaded our culture and affect the decisions we make. I sometimes hear people say they have these mindsets, and I admit I've had them too. In fact, I still experience them at times. Because they are so pervasive, it's important to recognize them and understand what they can do to your financial health, not to mention your emotional health.

Scarcity Mindset

A scarcity mindset is very common but many people don't even know they have it. (Yes, I know, I make it sound like a disease, and in some respects, it is.) It's a feeling of never having enough or thinking that there's never going to be enough to have what you want. If you grew up without much money or your parents always argued about never having enough money, you may have learned or been led to believe that money is in short supply or that you can lose it at any time. You may have also developed this mindset as an adult if you lost a job or lost a lot of money in the stock market.

When you have this kind of attitude around money, you think money is scarce or hard to come by. And when you do have some extra money, you're not really sure what to do with it. You tend to have an all-or-nothing response where you either hoard it for fear of not having enough or you spend it all because you don't know when or if you'll have it again. Either way, you end up with unhealthy money habits.

Poverty Mindset

Have you heard the term *poverty mindset*? It's very similar to the scarcity mindset and the two terms are sometimes used interchangeably. However, I do think they are a little different. The definition of poverty is the "state of being extremely poor" or "an inability to meet basic needs." It's also defined as "the state of being inferior in quality or insufficient in amount." The majority of us have no idea what it means to actually live a life of poverty. We are very fortunate to have access to many resources here in the United States, including food, water, and shelter.

A poverty *mindset* has to do more with the second definition and actually has *very little to do with income*. You can make a great income and still have a poverty mindset. Instead, it is a belief state that you are inferior or unworthy of having more money than you think you deserve, and what you think you deserve is very little. It's thinking in small terms and believing that you are not in control of your financial well-being.

People with this kind of mindset often complain about not having enough money and are jealous of those around them for what they have. They tend to blame others for their situation; blame the economy, stock market, or their income; and feel as though everything is out of their control. They sabotage themselves with their thoughts and words. For example, if you think that a minimum-wage job is the only one you can get or deserve to have, then you might have a poverty mindset. If you believe that you could never earn a certain kind of salary because it's just too crazy to even think about or you struggle with the idea of being "wealthy," you might have a poverty mindset. *People living paycheck to paycheck often have a poverty mindset to some extent.*

Both a scarcity mindset and a poverty mindset have to do with what you tell yourself about who you are and what you are worth. Most of the time, no one is telling you that these things are true except for *you*. These beliefs will unintentionally and yet inevitably keep you from achieving financial independence.

The Power of the Mind

There are many books, articles, quotes, and studies around the idea that you become what you think about. I'm not talking about the law of attraction here. I'm talking about the power of your mind and how amazing the brain is. I've always enjoyed reading self-help books. I remember back in my twenties reading *The Power of Positive Thinking* by Dr. Norman Vincent Peale. Many years later, I read a book called *Think and Grow Rich* by Napoleon Hill. There have been countless other books and articles that I have read on this topic, and what has always intrigued me is that what I think about on a daily basis can impact my life direction – and my financial future. The principle is that your brain believes what you tell it.

If you wake up in the morning and are already thinking about how you hate mornings, hate your job, don't like your coworkers, don't have any money, and wish you could take a vacation from your family . . . what kind of a day do you think you're going to have? That's right, probably not a very good one because you've already set yourself up for a bad day and trained your brain to think those negative thought patterns.

On the other hand, if you wake up in the morning and say to yourself, "I'm thankful to have another day, grateful to have a job that allows me to take care of my family's needs, blessed to have . . .," what kind of day do you think you might have, or at least start off with?

It's pretty easy for most people to think in negative terms, especially when it comes to money. You can probably come up with all kinds of reasons to be overwhelmed and stressed with your current situation. But where does that negative mindset get you? It puts you in a state of fear, confusion, victim mentality, and loss of control.

A scarcity or poverty mindset will keep you stuck in the mud and unable to move forward. It will stunt your financial growth, and it will leave you in the clutches of defeat.

But guess what? You can change that kind of mindset, and a negative mindset in general! You get to choose how you're going to think and what you're going to believe about money and your life. How? Stay with me because we're going to look at that in the next chapter. I will show you how to reset your money mindset so it's not one based on fear.

Your money story doesn't just stop. There isn't a "The End" until you leave this earth. You will continue to make good decisions and bad decisions around money. You will let others influence how you think and behave. You will encounter situations that make you think twice about what you believe to be true. The key is to be aware and recognize when it's happening. You are writing your story right now. How do you want it to end?

Spiritual Perspective

What have you been learning about God and money as an adult? Is it different from what you were taught as a child? Often, we don't think about how our Christian beliefs impact our thoughts around money, except maybe around the idea of giving and tithing. I'm very fortunate that I attend a church where the pastor speaks about money quite often and not just about tithing. Not all churches and pastors are comfortable around this topic as it is very personal and often emotional.

But, isn't church one of the best places for us to learn about how to manage our money according to God's Word? It's where we should be able to ask questions and find answers. What would God say about how you are managing your money right now? If that question sends pangs of shame and guilt down your spine, then maybe it's time to ask yourself why and what you want to do about it. Asking myself this question years ago was one of the turning points in my financial life. I knew in my heart that I wasn't being a good steward with what God had blessed me with. I decided it was time to change, and part of that change involved understanding my money story and rewriting it.

Did you identify with the descriptions of the scarcity or poverty mindset? I think we as Christians sometimes get stuck in a different kind of scarcity/poverty mindset when we think we're not good enough, we don't deserve to have more than someone else, or we are powerless to change our financial situations. For example:

Do you have a ceiling on your income? An amount that you are not comfortable going beyond because you're concerned what people in your church or community might think of you if you, as a Christian, made too much money?

Do you feel guilty for having too many things when you know that others have so much less?

Do you worry and complain about not having any money left at the end of the month but all you do to change your situation is pray and wait for God to take control and change it for you?

It's okay, you can say yes to any or all of these questions. There's no shame in acknowledging how you think and feel. I've been there too. The tug-of-war that goes on in my head about money is quite fierce. Sometimes, I feel guilty and unworthy for what God has blessed me with and other times I desire for much more (and feel guilty about that too).

I once heard someone say that God doesn't have a cap on His blessings for us, so why do we put a limit on what we think we can have? Is it possible that God wants us to have so much more than we think we deserve, including financial resources?

I've talked with people who really don't seem to believe they can do anything to change their situation. They pray and they wait for God to do something. Yes, God is in control, but he also allows us to make our own decisions. What if He is waiting for *you* to do something first? What if He's waiting for you to stop blaming and take responsibility for your decisions before He steps in to help?

Planning Your Escape

1. What experiences have you had as an adult that have made you feel ashamed or guilty around money?

2. How have you encountered a scarcity or poverty mindset? Do you recognize yourself in the descriptions found in this chapter?

3. How have you fought back against these traps?

CHAPTER 7

Hitting the Reset Button

I have a friend who told me that he never really cared about how much he was spending or how much debt he accrued or how little he had in savings because it didn't really matter. He didn't believe he was going to live past the age of thirty-six. He was convinced that he would die at a young age because that's what happened to his father. This mindset led him to spend without thinking and not plan for any future financial hurdles. His mantra was "I may as well have fun and spend what I have now because I may not be here to spend it tomorrow." Have you ever heard someone say that or maybe even said it yourself? It's not an atypical way of thinking.

Once my friend lived past the age of thirty-six, then forty and forty-five, reality began to sink in, and he realized that the story he had been telling himself for so long wasn't true. He may actually live much longer than he had anticipated. Uh-oh. Sadly, there was a mountain of debt and very little savings, plus a family to take care of. Moving forward, my friend was going to have to reset his way of thinking, believing, and living. But that was easier said than done because he had developed some unhealthy habits along the way that were difficult to change. Here are four steps that he needed to take when it came to resetting the story he'd been telling himself:

1. Acknowledge and accept that he might continue to live a longer life than he expected (and be grateful for it).
2. Forgive himself for the guilt and blame he felt over the financial position he and his family were in because of their overspending and lack of savings.
3. Change his thinking from "I probably won't live another five years" to "I could live another twenty years or more."
4. Create a plan and take immediate action to stabilize their current financial situation and provide for a better future. This might mean making some uncomfortable changes like getting a second job or a better paying one, finding a way to lower expenses, and becoming familiar with the words *no* and *wait* for both himself and his family.

Just as my friend had to come to terms with an old money story and resulting mindset that was no longer serving him well, you may have to do the same thing. When you are living paycheck to paycheck, struggling with debt, or just can't seem to manage your money the way you want to, you probably have some experiences or messages in your past that are holding you back.

It can be dangerous to hold on to a money story or mindset that is not serving you well. You stay stuck and miss out on a lot of potentially great opportunities. But, if that's true, what should you do about it? Let me offer a roadmap that can help.

Understand Your Money Story

First, get in touch with your story, from childhood to now. Become aware of what it is and accept it. Own it. If you haven't done the activities from the previous chapters trying to answer the questions and identifying the scenarios that you relate to, then go back and do that now. When you become familiar with your story, the messages you heard and the experiences you learned from, you begin to understand why you might be struggling with this whole money thing. And it opens the door to introduce your mind to a different way of thinking and believing.

Find Your Way to Forgiveness

Forgive yourself and others for the part they played in your story. It's easy to blame yourself or other people for your situation or the decisions you've made. You may have made some really poor spending or investment decisions. You may be blaming your ex for leaving you with a bunch of debt. Maybe you blame your parents for not teaching you how to manage money wisely or not being good role models. We all make mistakes and most of us have been victims of other people's mistakes. It's time to let go and move on. Accept that it WAS part of your story but now you're ready for a new one. Forgiveness isn't about forgetting the memories but about releasing them so you're not controlled by them. If you continue to fill your mind with negative messages, you will inevitably keep repeating the same behaviors that are contributing to the paycheck-to-paycheck lifestyle. Focusing on positive messages will steer you toward financial freedom.

Flip the script

Think about the one negative message that you keep telling yourself over and over and that you need to stop listening to. Here are some examples to help you:

- I'll always be broke.
- I need to work long hours to prove my strong work ethic.
- It's no use trying to save because something always happens and I end up having to spend it anyway.
- The man should make the bulk of the household income.
- I'll never be able to retire.
- I'll never be able to afford what I really want.

There are dozens more negative messages that we tell ourselves, tapes that repeat over and over in our heads. Take that negative experience or message and turn it into a positive one. Flip the script.

Here is how it works. Say you tell yourself that you've tried budgeting, but it doesn't work. You just can't stick with it; it's too tedious; and you hate budgeting anyway because it takes all the fun out of spending money. First, sticking to a budget can be difficult, but if you tell yourself that you can't do it because you've tried before and failed, then you've already set yourself up to fail again. So, flip the script and tell yourself you *can* do this budgeting thing because you're smart, capable, and confident. Second, instead of believing that budgeting takes the fun out of spending, think about how budgeting can actually allow you to spend *more*. What?! Oh yes, that's a lot more fun and a lot less stressful. We'll get to that later in the book.

Here are a few other simple script flips to consider:

Instead of saying:	**Say:**
I'll always be broke	I'll always be blessed
I'll never be able to afford . . .	How can I afford . . .
I can't stop spending money	I love watching my savings grow
I hate budgeting and the restrictions	I love budgeting and the freedom

The bottom line is to try and take those negative experiences and find the good in them; and change those negative thoughts into positive ones. This isn't an easy step, and it might take some time to figure out how to flip the script. If you need further help, you can find many blogs online that talk about how to change your money scripts.

Embrace Your New Story and Mindset and Take Action.

Your old story and ways of thinking weren't helping you develop and maintain a healthy relationship with money. What are you going to do differently now? How was your story or mindset holding you back and what can you do now to move forward? Your first step might be to post your new mantra someplace where you will see it and repeat it often.

You get to *choose* which story and mindset you're going to continue to follow. Just because you flipped a script in your head once doesn't mean your life or situation is going to change. Your old story and mindset will want to rule in your head again. So, you'll need to think on that new script often and develop new habits that go along with it.

How I Flipped My Script

As you read earlier, my money story impacted my work ethic with my believing that I needed to have more than one job to make ends meet. It impacted my spending habits, which ultimately led me into a good deal of debt. I've struggled with thinking that I shouldn't have too much money, and I've felt guilty when I looked at others who were less fortunate. Until I acknowledged these parts of my story and understood their impact on my relationship with money, I kept getting stuck. Once I started flipping the scripts in my head, I started to appreciate my previous positions and then change them to better ones.

For example, instead of thinking that I needed to have two jobs, I started thinking, "One job is sufficient to meet my needs." I had to face the fact that my problems were not income based (as my story led me to believe) but an issue of frivolous spending (a result of a different part of my story). My action plan involved creating some goals and developing different habits and priorities. I'm not going to lie. It was not easy. It typically takes a strong and healthy person to change their mindset. People stuck in brokenness or who don't really want to change are going to struggle more with this kind of activity.

Those old money stories and negative money scripts can make it difficult to get a handle on figuring out the right way to manage your finances. If you're living a paycheck-to-paycheck lifestyle, chances are probably pretty good that you didn't have someone sit down with you and explain how money works. Am I right? Did anyone ever talk to you about saving, giving, or investing? Or did you have to figure most of it out on your own? I've talked with adults who never learned basic money principles or how to read their credit card or investment statements, much less how to handle them responsibly.

For me, I learned the basics such as how to balance a checkbook and that it was good to put some money into a savings account. I knew how to count money and make change. Monopoly was one of my favorite board games, so of course I knew how to manage money better than most! The problem was that I never learned much about *why* giving, saving, and investing were important and how those things could impact my future. I really just thought that you save money to spend it later. I figured investing was for older people who were closer to retirement, and I was way too selfish to think of giving my money to anyone other than to myself (unless I was trying to impress someone). These were mindset issues that I eventually had to work through. And it's not that the thoughts were necessarily negative, but they definitely had a negative impact on my relationship with money.

Abundance and Wealth Mindset

In the previous chapter, you read about the scarcity and poverty mindsets. I want to close this chapter by briefly talking about flipping those mindsets to ones of abundance and wealth. This doesn't mean that I think we are all meant to be millionaires and have all the toys we want. Remember, these are mindset issues. It's not about the amount of money and stuff you have. Poverty, abundance, and wealth are all relative terms depending on your view and background. Although you may feel "poor," you are undoubtedly rich in someone else's eyes.

You can use similar steps to those listed earlier in this chapter to change your mindset away from feeling that money is scarce or that you're not worthy of having more of it. Let's look at one of my mindsets as an example. I've often struggled with the belief that it is selfish to have "too much money" or more than what I need to be content. Growing up without much money, hearing stories about how the poor are blessed, and feeling guilty for having "more" were all contributing factors to that belief. As I met people who had a lot more money than I did, I realized that I didn't think anything bad about them and began to question my long-held mindset. Maybe it's not wrong or selfish to "have more." Here is how I used the steps I told you about earlier to flip the script and reset my poverty mindset:

I reviewed my money story and determined what made me feel as if it was wrong and that I didn't deserve to have money in abundance. For me, this traced back to belief systems I learned in the church community and also the belief that people with a lot of money are selfish.

I forgave myself for my past mistakes and gave myself permission to release that story and my old mindset. I had to let go of the confusion and guilt that I had regarding the teachings around money that I learned. In my heart, I had to forgive the religious influencers in my life for focusing on the "blessed be the poor" type of speeches.

I flipped the script and turned my negative beliefs into positive ones. Instead of saying, "It's selfish to have more money than absolutely necessary," I started saying, "It's good to be able to bless others out of my abundance." Instead of saying, "I could never be rich," I started saying, "I will be rich." And instead of saying, "God hates the rich," I started saying, "God loves the rich and the poor equally."

I learned to embrace my new mindset and put it into action. I had to give "wealth" my own definition. I also had to get comfortable with the possibility that I *could* make a six-figure salary and that would not make me a bad person or any less "Christian" in God's eyes. Some may not think a six-figure salary denotes wealth, but that was the threshold that I had in my head that separated the wealthy from the middle class. Again, it was a mindset issue that I had to recognize didn't make a lot of sense and wasn't serving me well. I stopped spending so much money on stuff and started giving and saving more. The scariest thing I did was write down my dream income goal, and be comfortable with it.

Resetting a negative mindset can be difficult. You get comfortable with your belief systems and habits and might find them hard to change. You might not even know if you want to change them. The questions to ask yourself are, "Could any of these beliefs be holding me back from attaining the financial freedom I desire? Are they keeping me stuck in the paycheck-to-paycheck trap?" If you think the answers might be yes, then why not try to think a little differently and see what changes it brings.

In the next couple of chapters, we will take all of this information that you've been learning about your money story and money mindset and start to apply it towards escaping the paycheck-to-paycheck trap. In Chapter 8, we will look at the four areas that your money should be used for, and in Chapter 9, we will talk about many of the spending triggers that throw us off track when we're trying to reach a financial goal.

Spiritual Perspective

We spent a lot of time in the previous chapter's spiritual perspective section talking about your money mindset and how it relates to what you've learned in the church and through other spiritual influencers in your life. Now I want to focus on how you might need to do some of your own research as I had to do. The Bible stories around money that you heard and read growing up and that you've been holding on to – do you know the full context around them? Do you know what some of those parables really mean? I would encourage you to study them on your own if you haven't done that before.

What messages do you tell yourself about money and God or money and faith? Which messages are potentially holding you back from the blessings He may have in store for you? Do you need to reset your money mindset and flip some of those scripts so you can be an even better steward or servant?

Planning your Escape

1. What negative messages are you telling yourself that need to be reset?

2. Write the steps that you plan to take to reset your money mindset and flip the script. How can you change the words you tell yourself?

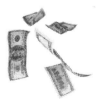

CHAPTER 8

The Balancing Act

You encounter and interact with money pretty much every day. Whether you are receiving a paycheck, paying a utility bill, going out to lunch, or picking up a penny that you found lying in the parking lot next to your car, you can see that money is all around. Unfortunately, it doesn't seem to *stay* around! In an effort to help you take control of your financial situation and stop living paycheck to paycheck, I want to talk about what to do with the money that you have coming in every month.

There are four main areas where money gets allocated: giving, saving, spending and investing. Most people don't think to include spending as one of those categories, but it's the largest one, so it absolutely needs to be included. All four of these areas should play a role in what we do with our money, but how? How do you balance these areas and not run out of money? When you're living paycheck to paycheck, you can barely afford everything that falls under Spending. Now, I'm telling you that you have to give some of that up in order to satisfy three more areas? You may think it's not possible, but it is.

When I speak at seminars and workshops, I like to ask the audience to write these four words – giving, saving, spending and investing – on a piece of paper, and leave a space next to each word. Then, without any more discussion, I ask them to write the percentage of their monthly net income (after taxes are taken out) that is allotted to each area.

I want you to do the same thing here. Next to each word, write the percentage of your income that goes into that category. This is not how much you think you *should* be contributing or *want* to be contributing, but how much you really are. It can include dollars that are being automatically deducted from your paycheck. If you are not contributing to that category, then the percentage is zero, and that's what you should write. There is no guilt or embarrassment here; you are the only one that will see these numbers.

Giving _____% Saving _____% Spending _____% Investing _____%

Good job! How do you feel about the numbers that you wrote down? Are you satisfied? Are you disappointed? Whatever you're feeling, it's okay. Even if you're satisfied, I encourage you to continue reading because I'm going to address each of these areas and share my recommendation of what your percentage should be. I know that you may not be able to adhere to these recommendations immediately, but they are the goals to strive for. Actually, these are *minimum* recommendations. *The less money you earmark to spending and the more you can allocate to the other three categories, the better.*

Giving (10%)

Giving is listed first for a reason. I believe it is foundational to financial success. We are truly blessed to have so much, especially here in the United States. Some people have a natural gift for giving while others struggle with this area. Our goal should be to give without expecting anything in return. There are various ways that we give. We can give our *time* by volunteering for events, cooking dinner for a family in need, teaching a Sunday school class, reading to a young child, or coaching a child's sports team. We can give of our *talents* by offering our expertise for free – for example, a landscaper offers to mulch the garden of an elderly neighbor. We can give of our *resources*, such as letting someone stay in our home when they have been temporarily displaced. Finally, we can give our *money*. The last one is what we will focus on, since money *is* the focus of this book. I have used a minimum of 10% of your income because (1) it's biblical and (2) it's what is widely recommended by other financial experts.

As we begin this section, let me ask you a few questions to get you thinking about this area of financial giving. As you read them, think about how your money story or money mindset may play a part in your answers and how they impact your attitude and the way you feel about giving.

Are you a financially giving person or desire to be? When someone is in need, do you jump in to help or do you wait to see if someone else will do it first? Do you give because you feel obligated? Or do you give with a joyful heart without expecting anything in return? Do you give because you want the recognition or do you give anonymously? Who or what do you want to give to? Your church? A favorite organization? A friend, neighbor or coworker in need?

I promise that when you start giving and making it the foundation of your financial budget, you will see amazing things happen. It doesn't have to be a lot. It may be only $10 to start. That's okay. The point is to start, and then get in the habit of doing it on a regular basis.

Finding room in the budget to give financially, especially when you're living paycheck to paycheck, can be difficult. I find that many people *want* to give or want to give more than what they are, but can't seem to be able to.

If you really want to give but are having a difficult time coming up with extra money, you may be going about it the wrong way. Here are a couple of recommendations that might help (it's what I do and it has helped me stay focused and consistent):

- First, most people wait until the end of the month to see how much money they have left over to give to their church or favorite charity. If you do it this way, you will rarely have the amount you want to give if you have anything left at all. Even if you have it in your budget, it's amazing how that money has disappeared before the month's end. Instead, of having your donation to be the last thing you do, consider making it at the beginning of the month, from your first paycheck.
- Second, think about automating your giving. Many charities and churches now have online giving where you can have your donation sent directly from your checking account and on a specific date. This is a great way to ensure you are meeting your goal. Just make sure you keep enough in your account to cover the transaction!

As you reflect on what giving means to you and how you want to incorporate it into your life, consider a few of my favorite quotes around giving and generosity:

- Generosity: The habit of giving freely without expecting anything in return. -Unknown
- We make a living by what we get, but we make a life by what we give. -Winston Churchill
- Sometimes when we are generous in small, barely detectable ways, it can change someone else's life forever. -Margaret Cho
- A man's true wealth is the good he does in this world. -Muhammad
- No one has ever become poor by giving. -Anne Frank

Saving (10%)

Whereas I believe that giving is foundational to managing your money, and we should all give to something (church or charitable organization), not everyone does. That's a choice. However, saving is something that absolutely every one of us needs to do. The problem is most don't. Why? Again, it's usually because there isn't any money left at the end of the month. Is this you? Do you have trouble saving even though you know you should?

There are different kinds of savings and people often get overwhelmed with trying to determine what to save for first. I often get asked the question, "Should I save for this or should I save for that?" "Should we save for college or save for our home repairs?" It's tough because there always seems to be something to save for, but there are also plenty of things that you need to pay for, and those tend to take priority. Nevertheless, if you want to escape the paycheck-to-paycheck trap, you must have savings.

Plan to save a minimum of 10% of your earnings each month. In a moment I will list the different types of savings you will eventually need, in order of their priority. People often want to jump out of order. For example, they want to save for a short-term expense instead of having the emergency fund in place. This is usually a mistake. Without that emergency savings, you are very susceptible to accumulating debt and living paycheck to paycheck.

One thing to remember before we look at the types of savings: *Saving is NOT the same thing as Investing!* They serve two different purposes. We'll talk about investing in the next section.

Initial Emergency Savings: This is $1,000 that you need to put in the bank and never touch unless you have a true emergency that you cannot pay for out of your budget. Keep this accessible, probably in your bank savings account.

Full Emergency Savings: This is a *minimum* of three to six months of expenses. You start saving this *after* you have paid off all your debt except for your mortgage. This is a buffer for larger emergencies or if you were to lose your job. If you are single, a one-income family or own a business, you might want to have a minimum of six to eight months saved since you are likely to be at more risk if something happens.

Short-Term Savings: This kind of savings is when you want to buy something like a new computer, appliance replacement, vacation, or similar purchase. It is something that you are usually going to save and then use to buy within the next year or two.

Long-Term Savings: This is for things that you will need to save for a longer period of time, usually three to five years or more. It may be for a down payment on a house, a car, a new roof, a wedding, and so on. You might consider putting this kind of savings into an online savings account where you can get a higher interest rate.

You will read more about savings throughout this book. Although you may not be in a position to save the 10% right now, you will be when you put the information from this book into practice.

Investing (10%)

In the previous section, I told you that saving and investing have two different purposes. You save so you can (1) have money to pay for emergencies and (2) accumulate money for purchases that you can pay for in cash. Investing, by comparison, is primarily for your retirement savings. You want to invest a minimum of 10%-15%.

Investing is the one area that seems to confuse most people. If you're going to get anxious or just not do something because you don't understand it, this is where it will happen. Why?

- **Lack of knowledge**. Many don't understand all the terminology that surrounds investing: equity stocks, growth funds, index funds, small-cap funds vs. large-cap funds, bonds, treasury bills, dividends, expense ratios, Roth IRAs, 401(k)/403(b), TSP, bull vs. bear market, and so forth. Need I say more? It can be downright overwhelming to even think about where or how to start.
- **Intimidation or Fear.** Investing is risky. What if you make a mistake and invest in the wrong thing and lose all your money? Better to not invest at all, right? Wrong! Don't let fear or intimidation paralyze you into inaction. Start small. Yes, you will probably make mistakes. I know that I have.

But I have also done some other things right that have paid off nicely.

- **Time.** We often think we have plenty of time to invest for retirement, but in reality, the sooner you start, the better. The longer you wait, the less time your money has to increase – and increase exponentially. That's what compound interest can do, and it is a miraculous thing to watch, especially when it's happening with your own money!

As intimidating as investing may seem, it's necessary to do. And once you begin to understand the terminology and put a plan into place, the decisions become easier and less time-consuming. We will talk about investing in more depth in Chapter 15.

Spending (70%)

Yes, you read that right. I have only 70% of your net income allocated to spending. Could you live on 70% of what you bring home every month? No way? How much did you allocate to the spending category in the earlier exercise? For me, it used to be pretty much 100%. I literally spent everything that I made and then some, which is how I ended up in debt. I used to *love* to spend money. Shopping for clothes and housing decor was a weekly adventure for me. Then I realized that my spending habits were keeping me trapped in a paycheck-to-paycheck lifestyle and I was tired of living that way. It took looking back through my checkbook and credit card statements to get a really good idea of how out of control my spending was.

Do you overspend most months? Do you typically get to the end of the month and have no money left? What causes that to happen for you? Clothes, home decorations, food, and mortgage . . . those were my leaks, the areas that I tended to spend the most money on. Generally, food is considered the most commonly overspent budget item, especially eating out. We eat out because we don't have time to cook, don't like to cook, don't want to cook, and it's a form of entertainment. We also spend a lot of money on "wants." We struggle with waiting and think we have to have everything right now.

In *Financial Recovery*, Karen McCall offers a "Do I need this?" challenge, which I love. She says "when facing a purchase decision and to see if it is a genuine need or impulsive want, ask yourself these three questions: (1) Do I really *need* this? (2) Do I *really* need this? (3) Do I really need *this*? Same question but pay attention to the italics. If yes to those three, then (4) Would buying this item be worth what I'd have to give up in order to get it?"[5] Did you catch that the first three questions are exactly the same, but a different word is emphasized, changing the meaning of the question?

What we need to watch is *how much* we spend and *what* we spend money on. Part of maintaining balance is in the area of spending. Ask yourself this question, "Are my spending behaviors causing me to live paycheck to paycheck?" Now I'm not going to tell you that you can't go out and have fun or spend money on yourself or your family. What I am going to do is ask you to be *aware* of your spending. That's it. Just be aware and open to possibly implementing a few changes.

We will talk a lot about spending in this book. In fact, the next chapter is devoted entirely to this category. From my own experience, and in my conversations with clients and others, I know that spending is generally the reason most have gotten into the paycheck-to-paycheck trap. If that's true for you as well, you won't be able to escape until you get a handle on it.

I understand these percentages may feel unrealistic to you at this point. However, I want you to see at the beginning that this is where we eventually want your money going. Once you escape the trap, keeping financial balance will help you stay out of the paycheck-to-paycheck lifestyle. It will allow you to give, save, invest, and spend wisely. It's not easy, but when you are incorporating all four areas into how you manage your money, you will feel more confidence, peace, and security.

Remember, the percentages that I gave you for giving, saving, and investing are the minimum. For most people, their money is going toward spending much more than any of the other three categories. You don't have to be like most people. I'm not, and neither are most others who are financially free. You can only do this if you put a stake in the ground and decide to get out of debt, stop spending on so many wants, and tell your money where you want it to go.

Now let's talk about those spending triggers . . .

Spiritual Perspective

When it comes to giving, most believers tend to automatically associate that with tithing to their church. That is a good thing. I firmly believe that you have been called to give to your home church first. The Bible says that we should give a tenth of what we have–10%. A majority of the people I talk with really want to give 10% to their church but just don't see room in their budget to be able to do it. Many of them are not giving anything financially. I once heard one of my pastors preach on this topic, and I remember him saying that tithing is not a salvation issue; it's a responsibility issue. We are responsible for helping our church family as best we can. I understand that you may not agree with what you think the money is being used for. But even if a portion of it is used for what you think it should be used for, I think it's worth it and what we're called to do.

There is debate as to whether the one-tenth should be out of your net or gross income. It is not clearly stated in the Bible and is therefore more of a personal issue. I choose to tithe on my gross income because I feel like that is what God has blessed me with. I feel like tithing after taxes have been taken out is not giving God all of my tithe. But, that's just me. You must decide what is right for you, and it doesn't make either one of us right or wrong.

Beyond the tithe, it is totally appropriate and recommended to support other causes and organizations that you believe in. I certainly do. Both my tithe and my other offerings are part of my monthly budget. Again, these other donations should come after your tithe to your church family.

We are called as believers to give, save, and invest our money. It's the wise and responsible thing to do. We have money and all our stuff because God has been so generous to us, even if we only have a little. We get so caught up in the spending category that we forget about the other three or just don't feel they are as important. The reality, however is those three areas are *most* important!

What would happen if believers around the world started giving more abundantly? What would happen in the church? In our neighborhoods? In our own families?

What would happen if believers started saving more and spending less? How would that help your family?

We are called to be role models for Jesus. I think learning how to balance our money and following through with it is a great testimony to those around us. What do you think?

Planning Your Escape

1. Go back to the beginning of the chapter where I asked you to write in the percentages that you think you contribute to each money role and write them again here. If you didn't do it, here's your chance to do it now.

Giving____% Saving____% Spending____% Investing____%

2. After reading this chapter, have you decided to change any of these percentages or do you hope to change your percentages in the near future once your debt is paid off? If so, write your new percentages here:

Giving____% Saving____% Spending____% Investing____%

3. When are you going to start your new balancing act? If you can't commit to the percentages that you ultimately want right now for whatever reason, how can you slowly increase each area?

CHAPTER 9

Your Spending Triggers

Spending money is what likely gets us into trouble and keeps us from staying within budget or achieving our financial goals. Whether it's for needs or wants, we have to spend money. There's no way around it, even for the extreme minimalist. But, many of us lack self-control over our spending habits. We let our emotions get in the way. We feel a sense of urgency to "buy now" or it will be gone forever. How many times have you bought something that you didn't even need just because it was too good of a deal to pass up?

Great marketers know how to capitalize on our emotions. They know how to create that sense of "I NEED this in my life NOW," even though you know you don't. They've learned specific behavioral strategies and marketing techniques that play on your scarcity mentality. Those coupons you get in the mail are thoughtfully designed to entice you to spend your hard-earned money. They tell you about how you really need the newly updated next best thing because it will run faster, last longer, and have a lot more gizmos to make life easier and more fun.

Do you remember the last time you got a flier in the mail from a dealership showing you pictures of the new cars that were out for that year? They also show you all of the new and cool luxuries available with that new car. I got one just a couple of weeks ago. Now, my car is nine years old and has just under 100,000 miles on it. When I get one of those fliers, my brain starts to stir and get excited. How fun would it be to have a nice new car with all the new accessories and new car smell? When I go to the dealership for service, I have to stay out of the showroom and not browse the parking lot. I know that if I start "browsing," I will start dreaming about "what if." But the reality is that I don't *need* a new vehicle right now. The one I have works perfectly fine, and I still love it. It just takes a while to remind and convince my emotions of that.

Here's a tip: Keep yourself away from temptation while you're trying to get a handle on your financial situation and you know you have a weakness for giving in! Don't look at those fliers if they are too tempting. Don't go through the car lot to "browse" the inventory. Don't open that email from your favorite store saying that you've received a 20% discount (there will *always* be a sale; you don't have to shop all of them). In fact, I recommend you unsubscribe from these emails if they're too tempting for you to resist. Don't drive through a new home tour unless you're actually looking for a new house.

I actually did the home tour thing a few months ago. I had gotten an advertisement in the mail about a new condominium neighborhood going up around the corner from me. Out of curiosity, I decided to go check it out. But I didn't just drive around. I went inside a couple of the homes. Big mistake! These homes were gorgeous! They were modern and clean, and the living rooms and kitchens were huge. I got back to my house and it just seemed so old and outdated. I was very tempted to put my house on the market and buy one of these beautiful condos . . . for about a week. Then sanity kicked back in. I love my house. It is paid for and I've lived in it for twenty years. Besides, if I decide to move, it will be to some place much warmer than northern Indiana!

Are you sensing how the spender personality in me can easily come out? Do you also see how I can put the brakes on and say no to myself? If you're a spender, you can do this too. It just takes some practice and self-restraint. You've got to acknowledge when you're in the midst of making a decision, recognize the emotions instigating the internal battle and then decide if the purchase is going to be worth it.

Aside from our emotions going haywire and the guru marketing strategies tapping into our scarcity mentality, there are various reasons why we overspend. I call them "spending triggers." The money story that you've learned about can feed into how your spending triggers developed.

In the following pages, I present ten spending triggers that I have identified through personal experience and work with my clients. Each has its own behavior or reasoning for why we succumb to it. As you read them, see which one best describes your reason for overspending.

Habit

Habits become part of our daily or weekly routine. They are things that we do almost unconsciously and without thinking. They can be good or bad. Good habits like brushing your teeth twice a day, waking up early to exercise, cleaning the house every Saturday morning, and creating a weekly or monthly budget help us lead more productive lives. We may not necessarily like doing them, but we know they're good for us and making habits out of them keeps us on track without us having to think too much about it.

Bad habits, such as smoking, gambling, overeating, or overspending, often keep us stuck and unable to move forward in making changes. Do you tend to reach for the can of soda when you know you should drink water, or sit on the couch watching your favorite show when you know you should exercise? We are creatures of habit and comfort even when it comes to our money. Do you whip out your debit card to pay for dinner even though you have cash in your wallet specifically designated for that purchase? Do you go to the grocery store every Wednesday night even when you don't really need anything? Do you go to your favorite restaurant every Friday night instead of cooking something at home? Do you buy your child a toy every time you go to the store? That last one is creating a habit for both of you.

These habits, like any others, can be difficult to break. One way to do it though is to simply be aware that you have a choice. Your habits do not have to control you. You get to choose how to use your time, talents, and money. The next time you are getting ready to engage in your bad habit, stop and ask yourself if it's the right decision. Do you really need to stop and get fast food on the way home from work?

Does your child really need another toy or game? Do you really need that big piece of chocolate cake? Hmmm . . .

Another way to break the habit is to interrupt it with a different behavior. In the book, *The Power of Habit*, Charles Duhigg talks about the transformative nature of keystone habits, the most important one being that of willpower.[6] Willpower becomes a habit by choosing a certain behavior ahead of time and then following that routine when an inflection point arrives. You decide ahead of time how you're going to react or respond to that particular situation.

For example, instead of going on your usual Saturday morning shopping trip, maybe you can go for a walk or read a book. Willpower helps make that choice a little easier. Not only does it break the cycle, but it also removes temptation, like we talked about earlier.

I'm Sorry

This trigger is not necessarily about buying your wife a bouquet of flowers because you did or said something wrong and you felt guilty. It's bigger than that. It's about consistently spending money you don't have to relieve a sense of pain. If you are divorced or widowed with young children, do you find yourself buying them extra stuff because you feel sorry or guilty that they don't have their other parent, and you're trying to make up for that loss?

Spending money on someone because you're sorry about something is not uncommon. The need to make things right or better sometimes drives us to spend more than we can afford. The reality is that you don't have to buy yourself out of guilt. Your spouse will most likely be happy with an apology and an I love you. Your kids just want you to spend time with them and be involved in their lives. Try it and see what happens.

Love

Love makes us do crazy things sometimes, including spending money we don't have! It might be buying something expensive for your significant other or spouse. It might be spending money on your children. Too often, we equate love with money. It's not even that we think we *have* to buy excessively for our loved ones; we *want* to. We want them to know how much we care about them. I mean, if your spouse buys you a blender or tickets to your favorite concert for your birthday, which one shows the most love? If your daughter is getting married, it's natural to want to find her the best wedding dress and have the best ceremony possible. There's nothing wrong with this – unless you don't have the money. Yes, you can put it on a credit card and figure out how you'll pay for it later. That's what most people do. But I don't want you to be like most people! I will show you how to have the best of both worlds coming up soon.

Appearances

Do you spend money to impress those around you? When was the last time you bought a new outfit for a date night or upcoming event? How much and how often do you spend money on spa treatments, nails, haircuts and dyes? Do you like to have the best "toys" or tools or the newest gadgets? Have you spent a lot more money on a new car or house because it would give you status and make you look like you have a lot of money? We love to be complimented and have people be impressed with our purchases. Spending money for appearance gives us that acknowledgment.

I used to do this one a lot. I would spend a bunch of money at my favorite department store knowing that the sales clerk would certainly be impressed with all my purchases. And I would wait for friends and coworkers to compliment me on those purchases. I would also spend extra money on a "pretty" new car that I knew would make me look good. Yes, I might have had a bit of an attention problem! Thankfully, I finally grew out of it.

I Deserve

Has your shopping buddy ever said to you, "Wow, that jacket looks great on you! You should get it. *You deserve it*!"? Our friends and loved ones are so kind to recognize our worthiness of such rewards. And we do the same thing for them. Although most don't come right out and say it, there is a well-developed attitude that we carry around which says "I work hard, so I deserve . . ." "I've had a really difficult week/month/year, so I deserve . . ."

Once again, I've been there and done that. Sometimes, it's something really small like I deserve this ice cream cone even though I will have to run five miles to balance out the calories. Other times, it's a new outfit or dinner at an expensive restaurant. The ones that get us into even more financial trouble are larger expenses like a vacation or a new car.

Is it wrong to feel deserving of such things? No, I don't think so. You do work hard and sometimes you do have a really challenging time that you've gone through. We need those rewards to refresh us and keep us going. Not all rewards cost money, but when they do, you want to build those rewards into your overall financial plan.

Later in this book, I'm going to show you how to do that without it making you feel guilty or causing you stress.

Kids' Clothes and Toys

Be honest . . . how many times do you find yourself picking up "something little" for your child or grandchild? You find the cutest little outfit and just have to buy it. Your grandson mentioned that he wanted a certain toy, and you just happened to see it in the store that you were in, so you bought it. After all, it didn't cost very much. The problem is that all of these "little gifts" can clog up your cash flow. If you know that buying stuff for your kids and grandkids is a trigger for you, then you will want to include it in your spending plan..

Giving

This trigger hits home if you find yourself always helping *others* financially. You take the idea, "it is better to give than to have or receive" to heart. My mom is an example of a giver. She is one of the first ones to cook something and take it to a neighbor in need. If she finds out that one of her kids or grandkids needs something, she will offer to pay for it or just go and buy it. If we go to dinner, she always wants to pay for it. She's been a great example of what giving to others looks like.

Giving is an awesome thing to do with your money. However, when taken to extremes, it can lead some people into a financial hole. If you are in debt but still picking up the tab when you're out with family or friends, you're going to end up digging a deeper financial hole. If you are constantly donating to charitable organizations because you get that tug on your heartstrings, but you can't put food on the table for your family, you are not being a good example to your children. I don't want you to stop giving, but I do want you to give out of your abundance and not out of guilt, appearance, or the potentiality of affecting your family's basic needs.

Boredom

How many times do you find yourself shopping because you're bored? You're early for an appointment and figure you'll just stop in to the little shop next door to bide your time. Or you need to go pick up something at the home improvement store, but you're not really in any hurry so you walk up and down all the aisles just to see if there's anything else you might be forgetting that you "need." Or you're at home relaxing and browsing online while watching television. Even if you have no intention of buying anything, you find a sweet little deal that is just too good to pass up. And then you find another great deal. And before you know it, your boredom or waiting time has just cost you *money*. Been there and done that more times than I can count! This is another situation where removing temptation is key.

Addiction

It's time to get serious with this one. Too many people are living paycheck to paycheck and unable to meet their financial needs and goals because they are spending money on an addiction. *Psychology Today* states that an addiction is "a condition in which a person engages in use of a substance or in a behavior for which the rewarding effects provide a compelling incentive to repeatedly pursue the behavior despite detrimental consequences."[7] From substance abuse with tobacco, drugs, or alcohol to behaviors around compulsive spending, gambling, or pornography, the addiction will almost always cost you money and prevent you from attaining financial freedom.

These addictions can be very dangerous to your health and your finances. One family that I talked with was barely able to pay their utility bills each month. When I saw them out in their car not long after our meeting, I saw them lighting up their cigarettes. Now, I'm not judging them for smoking, but I couldn't help but wonder how much they were spending on that addiction when that money could be better served by paying their bills. My shopping habit actually became an addiction. I was addicted to the high of finding a sale, of getting attention, and the temporary adrenaline rush that I got from it. I spent *so* much money during that time, money that I could have been using to pay off debt.

If you are engaged in any kind of addictive behavior, please find a safe person to talk with and get some help. It's time to take control and put this very risky habit to rest.

Experiences, Adventure, Entertainment, or Hobbies

The name of the game here is *fun*! Do you love to travel or attend special events? For many of my clients, vacations are a huge budget buster. They want to go skiing in Colorado, take the family to Disney World, or visit relatives on the other side of the country. Great! I want you to be able to have these amazing adventures, but only if you have saved for them and they are not causing you emotional stress and keeping you stuck living paycheck to paycheck. Think about your last vacation. How much did you spend altogether with hotel, food, airfare or gas, and experiences while you were on that vacation? Okay, so maybe you got to stay with family and didn't have to pay for a hotel or food. What *did* you pay for?

Experiences like attending movies, concerts, and sporting events also fall under this category, as well as hobbies where you have to pay to play, like golf, for example. These can cost a lot of money, especially if you're engaging in them often and paying for more than just you. Besides the cost of tickets (which can be crazy expensive in itself), you're also usually paying for some food and drink, as well as gas or airfare, if you're traveling outside of your home city or state.

Are you an avid reader and enjoy buying new books? Do you enjoy landscaping, woodworking, sewing, and other crafts? How much money have you spent on these hobbies lately?

Are you the one who likes a good party and loves to entertain? Do you enjoy having family and friends over for holidays or just to get people together? Some people are great hosts and hostesses and they take great joy in creating these events. However, you might find yourself playing hostess too many times or in a grandiose way. The cost of all that food and the related decorations and other things can become burdensome, especially if you're doing it all yourself. Asking your guests to bring something to share so you're not responsible for everything is one step in the right direction. It can help with the expenses and also free up some of your time.

Again, I want you to be able to do these things, but be wise about it. Plan and budget for them. It will make the experiences and hobbies much more enjoyable and less stressful later.

So, which trigger resonates with you? Do you see how your spending triggers can impact your financial success? Now that you know what is holding you back, what are some steps that you can take to move forward? What can you do to remove temptations? Answer these questions under the Planning Your Escape activity section.

In the next chapter, we will talk about creating goals and how to align them with your values so you are more inclined to accomplish them. When you have a financial goal that you are striving for, it can curb the temptation and desire to give in to your spending triggers.

Spiritual Perspective

God grants us the ability to earn a paycheck and make our own decisions about what we're going to do with that money. That is awesome and scary at the same time because He also created us as emotional beings, so our judgment gets cloudy sometimes. The triggers presented in this chapter can easily throw us off course and keep us from the blessings that He wants to give us. Think about that for a minute. What blessings might you be missing out on because you are overspending in one or more of these areas?

Planning Your Escape

1. Which spending trigger(s) did you find yourself saying "That's me" to?

2. How has your money story impacted or developed your triggers?

3. How is giving in to your spending triggers keeping you stuck living paycheck to paycheck?

4. What specific steps are you going to take to remove temptation so you can move forward? For example, what stores do you need to stay away from or what emails do you need to unsubscribe from?

CHAPTER 10

Goals, Values, and Your Why-What-How

When I was struggling with debt and trying to get my financial life in order, I found it much easier to be successful when I had a goal in mind *and* when it aligned with my core values. For example, when I decided that I wanted to have three months of expenses in an emergency fund, I got creative in making some extra income and didn't give in to my spending triggers as much because I wanted to make that goal. Similarly, when I decided that I wanted to have my house paid off and be completely debt free, I gave myself a date to get it accomplished. Having a date pushed me to be more conscious of my spending decisions and made my goal more concrete. Both goals had become part of a newly found value of not wanting to owe anyone anything. In this chapter, I explain how you can set your own achievable goals, financial and otherwise.

Set Achievable Goals

We make goals for all kinds of things. Students make goals about what kind of grades they want to get in their classes. As adults, we set goals for our careers, marriage, kids, business, how much money we want to make, and when we want to retire. We set goals for things we want to do, like lose weight or take a vacation, or things we want to buy, like a house or new car. January is known as the time to set resolutions for another year and click the restart button for the ones that weren't accomplished the year before. Think about that word *resolutions* for a minute. What does it really mean? It means that you resolve or decide to do something. Linking these two concepts together, you make resolutions to accomplish your goals.

Some people are really good at making resolutions and setting goals; others struggle with this practice or don't really see the need for it. Those who do participate often make goals that are too general. For example, you might say that your goal is to save more money this year. Great . . . but what does that mean? How much money and by what time? Is it the $1,000 starter emergency fund? Or is it six months of living expenses? Do you want to have it saved in three, six, or twelve months? By being specific, you will make it much easier to determine whether you are on track to meet your goal. It's one part of the acronym that you've probably heard about how to establish an achievable goal; it needs to be SMART (specific, measurable, attainable, relevant, and time-bound).

Making resolutions and setting goals is important. It gives you direction and a sense of purpose. It helps you think about where you want to be and what you want to do in the future, both in the short term and in the long term. Some people create written lists of their goals. Others design something like a vision board that has pictures and words representing what they want to have and achieve. Both provide a place for you to always see what you're hoping to accomplish.

But goal setting can also be challenging, and it's not unusual for people to try it a couple of times and then quit. Think about these three questions:

1. Do you make resolutions and then find yourself getting sidetracked from them?
2. Do you start out with really good intentions to get something done and then give up halfway through?
3. Do you get frustrated when you don't meet your goals?

I have said yes to all of these questions. Whether it is a goal for my physical, social, professional, spiritual, or business well-being, sometimes I struggle to attain it. So, what is the problem and what can we do about it?

One reason I think we struggle with attaining our goals is that we don't create a plan. Have you ever heard the saying, "A goal without a plan is just a dream"? We can dream about and wish for things all we want, but if you don't develop a specific plan of what your goals are and how you are going to attain them, they probably aren't going to happen. For example, you can set a goal to stop eating snacks at work (both a health goal and a money goal), but if you don't determine what steps you're going to take when the urge to snack comes on, you're probably going to give in. A few more times, and then you just give up on that goal and think maybe you'll try it again another time. In addition to the planning component, let's look at another consideration for why we can't seem to stay on track with our goals that were so important to us at the time we created them.

Explore Your Why-What-How

I believe we struggle to keep our resolutions or don't meet our goal expectations because we haven't identified our Why, What, and How, and that is what I want to focus on here. Knowing your Why-What-How is the first step when determining what your goals are. It gets you thinking on a deeper and more emotional level. It gives you a reason for doing what you say you want to do. When deciding on a goal or resolution, ask yourself these three questions:

1. Why is this goal important to me?
2. What will accomplishing this goal do for me and my family?
3. How will this goal change me or my situation for the better? How will I feel when I have met this goal?

You may notice the three questions are closely aligned. Each question can be used to further and more deeply explore your motivation for attaining your goal. You don't necessarily have to answer all of them for each goal that you are creating. The point is to get clear on your reasons for achieving the goal, because when you get tired or frustrated, you will want to come back to your answers to these questions for continuing motivation. So, use whichever questions will help you do this best. Now let's look at a specific example of using all three questions, so you can see how it works.

Let's say that you have a very broad resolution to stop living paycheck to paycheck (that's why you're reading this book, right?). My questions to you would be: Why is that goal important to you (e.g., I wouldn't be stressed, wondering if I have enough money to pay the bills every month)? What would you be able to do if you weren't living paycheck to paycheck anymore (e.g., I would be able to save more and take a vacation without feeling guilty)? How would it feel to have positive cash flow at the end of the month and how would it change your life (e.g., I would feel more secure and able to sleep again)?

It's easy to create a list of general dreams and ideas that we want to do, see, or have. I can come up with twenty easily. But to actually make one of these ideas into a concrete and achievable goal takes a lot more work. You have to define the goal, give it a deadline, and make sure that it is something that you can actually attain. You probably won't be able to become a millionaire in ten years if your income is $30,000 *and* you're a chronic spender. It also has to mean something to you. Otherwise, it is likely to stay just a dream or nice idea.

When you have you Why-What-How, you have a built-in motivator to help you achieve that goal. It's not always easy to come up with the answers. Sometimes you have to ask yourself the questions more than once. Many of my clients struggle with some level of debt that they want to get rid of. So, I will often ask them (a) why is getting out of debt important to them, (b) what would they be able to do if they didn't have debt, and (c) how would they feel to be finally be debt-free? They usually start off with things like "I'm tired of not having enough money at the end of the month," "I want to get my credit score up so I can buy a house," or "I just want to feel some peace about the future." They are good answers, but I often wonder if there is more. So, I ask them the questions again. And maybe again.

Until I get them to say what is really at the core of wanting to change their behaviors. "I want to be able to sleep at night without the stress of wondering which creditor will be calling me tomorrow and to feel in control of where my money is going." "I want to take my family on vacation, so we can spend quality time together and not worry about how much money we're adding to debt because we will be free from that stress." These are reasons that keep us motivated to achieve success.

Here are some more examples of goals and the W-W-H's behind them. These do not necessarily answer all three questions and are not intended to be SMART goals. Rather, they illustrate common motivators for people with concrete goals:

- Lose thirty pounds because you want to be able to play ball with your kids, look amazing in your wedding dress, or curb a potential medical issue
- Pay off all credit card debt in two years because you are tired of losing money to interest and late fees and want to start saving
- Meet with an estate attorney to create your will so you can be confident that your property and assets will go exactly where and to whom you want
- Start your own business so you can spend time doing what you are passionate about and have more flexibility
- Spend thirty minutes each morning in quiet reflection or prayer because you want to start the day with a sense of calm and peace and talking with God
- Do five unassisted chin-ups because it will prove that you have great upper-body strength (This is one of my goals that is still unattained but a work in progress.)

Determine Your Core Values

Part of knowing your Why-What-How is knowing what your *core values* are. What is important to you? What do you take a stand for? Your values may come from what your parents taught you or experiences that you've had. These may be personal values such as honesty, integrity, trust, and love that are character traits we expect from ourselves and others. Or they may be values like friendship, family, balance, independence, and security. Our core values help dictate our choices. When we make a decision that is not in line with one of our values, we feel tension. For example, you may have missed your child's school or extracurricular activity because you had to work and then felt disappointment and frustration at not being there. That's because you encountered a conflict with your core value of spending time with your kids.

I once read something that has stayed with me for a long time. It said to look at your checkbook and see where you've been spending most of your money. If you're one of the many people who doesn't own a checkbook anymore or very rarely uses one, then look at your bank and credit card statements. Where is the bulk of your money going? Your mortgage? Food? Car Payments? Amazon or a department store? Now ask yourself this question: *does that match your core financial values*? If one of your values is generosity, is that evident in how you spend your money? Or has it been a few months (or years) since you last gave to your church or favorite charity? If you value simplicity and don't like to spend a lot of money on fancy restaurants, then you're going to feel tension when you go with friends who like to eat at those places. On the other hand, if you value luxury, then flying economy or staying at a cheap hotel is going to make you feel stressed. We all have different values. Knowing yours will help you set better goals and make better decisions, resulting in less angst.

Position Your Goals

It's important to write down your goals along with your Why-What-How so that you can return to them as needed. Personalize them in a way that resonates with you. Your W-W-H does not need to be formal; just make sure it reminds you of why you want to achieve this goal. If you don't do well with words and would like a more visual reminder, then find pictures that depict your Why just as you would do for a vision board. Some people like to do a thermometer-like visual for their goal that has different steps listed and you can check off or color the steps after you accomplish them.

I recommend posting your goals and your Why-What-How where that you will see them every day. In fact, post them in more than one place. Put them on the refrigerator, your mirror in the bathroom, the dashboard on your car, or in a reminder app on your phone. If your goals and W-W-H are not constantly in front of you, they will be much more difficult to achieve.

As you work through this, aim to have some short-term goals and some long-term ones. I consider short term less than two years, which might include things like saving for a vacation, losing weight, buying a new appliance, or starting a part-time business. Long-term goals might include getting married, having kids, saving for a down payment on a house or college, making the part-time business go full-time, or retirement. You might also have goals that are daily, weekly, or monthly behaviors that you haven't been doing but want to. Examples are tracking receipts every day, creating a spending plan every month, exercising three times a week, calling five business prospects every day, and watching television two hours per night instead of five. These are the easiest to find either success or failure with because they happen so frequently.

Don't Give Up

One last thing that I want you to think about. Knowing your Why-What-How will prompt you to move and take action when you start feeling stuck, get distracted, or want to give up. When you notice these challenges, ask yourself *why*. Why are you feeling stuck? Why are you getting distracted? Why do you want to give up? If you're struggling with why, then ask *what*. What is keeping you stuck? What is distracting you? What is keeping you from moving forward? Is it a time issue, lack of resources, lack of motivation? Go back to your Why-What-How and your core values. Do your answers to those questions still hold true? Or have they changed? Is your goal truly aligned with one of your core values? Is there someone who can help you get back on track or hold you accountable?

You might struggle with your goal because it is too broad or too big. In that case, try to break it down into smaller goals. For example, let's say you set an initial goal in January to save $3,000 by the end of the year. By March, you only have $200 saved and feel that it is hopeless to make your goal, so you're ready to just give up. First, let's do a few things.

Take a look at what has gotten in your way up to this point. Did you make a specific plan on how to save this money (e.g. save $250 per month) or was it just a general idea of saving here and there? Did the amount you planned end up not being realistic or did you just keep spending it before you could save it?

Re-evaluate whether the goal is still important to you and why. Go back to the W-W-H discussion to come up with a new one if needed.

With three-fourths of the time left, determine if you still want to try to save the $3,000 or if you need to cut it in half (or more). There's no shame in re-adjusting a goal.

Set a new monthly amount and have it automatically deducted from your paycheck and sent to your savings account. What you don't have immediate access to is less likely to be spent!

Find a way to hold yourself accountable every month and build in a reward system for each month that you have successfully saved your goal amount.

Creating goals and understanding your Why-What-How and core values are just the first steps. You still need to have a plan outlining what you're going to do to achieve them and what you're going to do when you hit a roadblock. The next few chapters will help you in creating a financial plan that allows you to escape the paycheck-to-paycheck trap.

Spiritual Perspective

Did you know that the Bible talks about goal-setting and values? Consider Luke 14:28 which says, "Suppose one of you wants to build a tower. Won't you first sit down and estimate the cost to see if you have enough money to complete it?" Some Christians don't believe in goal setting because they think that we should rely solely on God's direction. But we see here that having a goal and creating a plan to attain it is Biblical.

Wouldn't our prayer lives be more productive if we invited God into our goal-setting process knowing that we must be willing to change our goals if we believe God is calling us in a different direction later?

Planning Your Escape

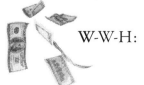

1. Write down two or three goals and your Why-What-How for each of them. At least one of your goals should be a financial one. Make sure your goals are specific, measurable, and attainable at the very least. Also, make sure your W-W-H is your true deep emotionally-connected reason for achieving that goal. You may need to ask yourself the W-W-H questions two or three times to make sure you've really delved into the possibilities.

   Goal 1:

   W-W-H:

   Goal 2:

   W-W-H:

   Goal 3:

   W-W-H:

2. When you face challenges in trying to achieve your goals, what usually gets in your way? Why do you usually get distracted or give up? Think about the last time this happened for you and write what happened here or on one of the note-taking pages in the back of the book:

3. What can you do next time you encounter challenges that get in the way of achieving your goals? How can you stay on track? Who can help you?

4. Consider the values listed below. On a scale of 1 to 5 (1-lowest, 5-highest), mark what kind of value each one holds for you. If you can't find yours in the list, write them on the blank lines.

___ Time with family
___ Eating out
___ Taking an annual vacation
___ Watching television
___ Providing for your family
___ Safety and security
___ Friendships
___ Career
___ Financial freedom
___ Physical appearance
___ Hobbies and Recreation
___ Exercise
___ Generosity
___ ____________________
___ ____________________
___ ____________________

PART II

Six Steps Toward Financial Freedom

CHAPTER 11

Create Your Escape Plan

In the previous chapter, we looked at setting goals that have specific meaning to you and align with your core values. We talked about how difficult it is to fulfill your dreams and attain your goals if you do not have a plan of what specific steps you are going to take and what behaviors you need to change.

Now it's time to focus on one specific goal – to escape the paycheck-to-paycheck trap – and design a plan that will help you achieve it. But I have a surprise for you. There is a second goal we are going to look at, because I don't want you to just stop living paycheck to paycheck. I want you to go beyond that. So, your next goal after you stop living paycheck to paycheck is to begin walking toward financial freedom.

In the next few chapters, I will share six steps you need to take to reach both of these goals. Steps 1 through 4 will help you to achieve the first goal. Steps 5 and 6 will be instrumental in directing you toward attaining the second one. Are you excited?

Here is a quick look at each step:

- Step 1: Prepare for the Inevitable – you will learn how to create your initial emergency fund as quickly as possible
- Step 2: Take Your Money Snapshot – you will see what your financial picture really looks like and create a spending plan
- Step 3: Get Out of the Well – you will create a plan to get out of debt
- Step 4: Save a Minimum of 3-6 Months' Expenses
- Step 5: Save 15% of Your Income
- Step 6: Create Additional Savings Buckets and Pay off Your Mortgage

Even if you look at the chapter headings and think this is nothing new and what you've heard before, read them anyway because you will get my take on it. Maybe you'll finally take action on what you think you already know but still haven't put into practice. I spent years hearing and reading about what I should do while still doing what I *wanted* to do. What changed? I finally got tired of the emotional stress and started considering the real possibility that I would never be able to quit working if I kept going the way I was. I wanted *options*. I wanted to be in a position where I was making money while I slept (that's called passive income and it's amazing . . . but more on that in Chapter 15!). I also wanted to be able to start my own business and take vacations without worrying about how to pay for it all.

What about you? Do you want to create options for yourself? Then, let's get started and remember to keep an open mind.

Planning Your Escape

1. If you haven't come up with your Why-What-How for escaping the paycheck-to-paycheck trap, then I'm going to ask you to do that here. Think about how being free from that would change your life and then answer these questions:

- Why is this goal important to me?
- What would I be able to do with extra money that I have left at the end of every month?
- How will I feel to not have to worry about whether I will have enough money to pay that last bill at the end of the month or for one more run to the grocery store?
- How does not living paycheck to paycheck align with my core values?

2. Remember, it's also important to post your goal and your W-W-H in a prominent place and determine a plan of action to combat the exhaustion or frustration that so often comes when reaching for a goal.

- Where will you post your goal and W-W-H statement?

- What kind of visual will you use to track your progress (e.g., a check-off list for each step or a thermometer)?

- What obstacles do you foresee that may hinder or derail you from reaching this goal?

- Who can you talk to who will encourage you and help you get back on track? Write that person's name here:

Good job! Now let's move on to Step 1 . . .

CHAPTER 12

Prepare for the Inevitable

Are you ready? In this chapter, I present Step 1 in the plan to escape the paycheck-to-paycheck trap and achieve financial freedom. This six-step process begins with a small goal that you can reach in just a matter of months. It's the emergency fund, and it is an essential component of your plan. It sets the foundation for getting out of debt and supersizing your savings. Here's what my clients Tony and Corey learned about the importance of having an emergency fund.

When I met Tony and Corey a couple of years ago, they were feeling frustrated and angry with each other for the financial situation that they were in. They were tired of living paycheck to paycheck but didn't know how to get out of the trap. At the time, they didn't have anything in a savings account and only had a small balance in their checking account. We worked together on a plan, and their first step was to put some money in an emergency fund. They were proud of themselves when they got this accomplished in a few months. Soon after, Tony had to take his car in for a transmission issue. Although they were disappointed to have to use money from the emergency fund that they had painstakingly accumulated, they were glad that they had the money to pay cash and didn't have to add more to their debt load. They learned the importance of having money in a savings account that is earmarked specifically for an emergency.

Step 1: Start Your Emergency Fund

You may have heard about how you should have this little thing called an emergency fund. Some call it a rainy day fund or a DNT (do not touch) fund. Call it what you want, but if you don't have at least $1,000 in an emergency fund, that should be your first financial goal within this plan. If you're on a fixed or lower income, you might be able to get away with a minimum of $500. If you're a single parent or your sole income is from a solo business, you might want closer to $1,500. Your WHY for this goal is to have some money put away for those times when a minor curveball comes along tempting you to go off-course. It *will* happen, and you want to be able to pay cash if possible and not have to use a credit card, especially if you already have credit card debt.

I know that it can be a challenge to accumulate that $1,000. And it's even more difficult to *keep* that $1,000 just sitting there! Because, sure enough, as soon as you get close to having your emergency fund in place, *something* is going to happen. All that hard work at saving is gone, and you barely blinked. It's so frustrating! And more so because you know you have to replenish it. But remember, that's what it's for. This may have been the first time that you didn't have to stress about how you were going to pay for a crisis. You had the money. Yes, you have to start over, but that's better than not having started in the first place.

There are a lot of ways that you can get this money and get it fast, but I find that many still struggle to get it done. Some have trouble committing to it and can't embrace the Why behind it. Others always seem to have a crisis happen before they can even get their fund together and they just give up. Nevertheless, you have several options for how to build your fund quickly if you are willing to make some temporary shifts in time management and behaviors:

- Put money into savings with your first paycheck each month. If you wait until the end of the month you'll never have enough because it will already be spent on something else.
- Have your employer or bank transfer a set dollar amount automatically from your paycheck to your savings account (This direct deposit is likely the easiest way to save money).
- Sell stuff through a garage sale at your house or online. In my city, we have local garage sales online, and people are buying and selling items all day every day. Many people have also been successful selling items through sites like Craigslist or eBay. (I have no experience with these sites and am not necessarily recommending them.)

- Send any extra money – bonuses, gift money, tax refund – straight to your savings account.
- Get a temporary part-time job. Go to work for your favorite department store. Deliver pizza or groceries. Sign up with a temporary service for evening positions. Mow some lawns or snow-blow some driveways. Just yesterday, I saw that a neighbor posted on our community Facebook page that he would power wash your house for a set price. What a great idea! Yes, he would have to get the equipment necessary to do this, but after that, it's all profit.
- Donate plasma if you live in a bigger city that offers this. This is a great way to make some extra money *and* help someone in need.
- Re-evaluate your expenses. Are you paying for a gym membership or subscription that you no longer use? Can you lower your cell phone or cable bill? Can you cut your morning coffee/donut run to two days instead of five? Do you have too much taken out of your paycheck so you can have a bigger tax refund? Do you have money in a cash value life insurance policy? (Look into closing the account and get term insurance instead.)
- My favorite one: Put yourself and your family on a spending freeze. Take thirty days and do not spend any money on anything that is not an absolute necessity. That means no shopping trips except for groceries, no eating out, no new toys for the kids, and no entertainment that costs money. Be sure to plan for that month ahead of time. If your kids are involved in sports or other activities, you will need to have kept a little money aside to pay for these things. I think you might be

surprised by how much you saved at the end of the month. I still put myself on spending freezes when I'm trying to meet a financial goal in a short period of time. The money that I save from not buying clothes, household items, pet toys, and eating out is always substantial, and often more than I would have thought.

- Check out the resources in the back of this book and search online for ways to make extra money; you will find lots of ideas.

If you find that you need to dip into the emergency fund for some reason, make sure that it is truly for an emergency. You need to decide ahead of time what that means for you. However, I will tell you that wanting a new outfit for a date does not qualify (sorry!). Neither does buying a new television, new furniture, or back-to-school clothes for the kids. These types of purchases should be saved for and then made when you have the cash to pay for them. Use one of the strategies listed earlier to accumulate extra cash in the short term.

If you are married, you and your spouse should agree on what constitutes an appropriate withdrawal from this fund together. I have worked with many couples who have their fund established and then one of them dips into it without telling the other (usually for a non-emergency purchase). You can imagine the resulting anger, frustration, and mistrust. Maybe you've even been there. If the two of you have a habit of not communicating with each other about money or one of you tends to make all of the money decisions, this is where you need to begin to shift your habits. You need to become a team and create this emergency fund together and then agree on what kinds of withdrawals from it will be appropriate. Notice that I didn't say what would be *allowed*. That's because that word has a parent or bossy connotation to it and I want you to be partners, not parent-child.

Ultimately, your emergency fund is for those unexpected, unpredictable, and immediate needs. Very few things actually qualify because most expenses are predictable; a job loss is one that fits all three categories. There will always be car repairs, home repairs, doctor's appointments, and so forth. Eventually, you will have enough cash flow to create savings "buckets" for these things. (Chapter 16 goes in-depth on how to protect yourself and your finances from these upsets.) If you're not at that point yet and you need help determining what can be called an emergency, here are some examples:

- Your *only* car gets a flat tire or has some other issue making it dangerous to drive it. If you have more than one car in the family, then it's time to carpool for a while.
- The furnace or air conditioner stops working in freezing or severe hot temperatures. Otherwise, it is very possible that you can wait a little while and save up some money for the service call or replacement. I know many people who have done this, including myself. It may be a little uncomfortable, but it's doable.
- You have to make an unexpected trip to the doctor's office for an emergency.
- Your fur-child (also known as a pet) has to go to the vet for an emergency. This is not for a routine check-up.

Again, keep in mind that none of these are entirely unpredictable – even a medical emergency can be planned for – so they technically should be areas that you are saving for in a separate account, not coming out of your emergency fund. However, when you are just starting out with a savings account, these are the types of events that may warrant a withdrawal.

One last thing . . . I know it's tempting to use some of your emergency fund to pay down debt. Please do not do this. Yes, it's hard to have $1,000 just sitting there doing nothing when you could use some of it to pay off one of your credit cards, and it feels counterintuitive to leave it alone. Remember that at this beginning stage, your emergency fund is there so you won't add even more to your debt and to keep your anxiety levels low. Call it another insurance policy if you will.

Spiritual Perspective

Having an emergency fund is a wise and godly step in beginning to manage your money. You have a responsibility to be prepared for emergencies, especially if you are a caregiver, and are called to be a good example to your children in all ways, which includes finances.

Without this fund, you will continue to end up in bondage to debt or at the very least not allowing your money to work for you in the most efficient way possible.

Planning Your Escape

1. How will you fund your initial emergency fund?

2. Define what the emergency fund will be used for. Discuss with your significant other to ensure you are in agreement.

3. Define what the emergency fund will *not* be used for. Discuss with your significant other to ensure you are in agreement.

CHAPTER 13

Take a Money Snapshot

While you work on quickly getting that emergency fund in place, you also want to take the time to look at what's really going on with your money. You want to know what is coming in (income sources) and what is going out (expenses). *Awareness* is what this step is all about, and it is absolutely critical to your plan.

Step 2: Create Your Spending Plan

You probably know how much you generally bring in every month if you have a regular paycheck. However, if you are on commission or have your own business, your income may be inconsistent. Either way, you may feel that your money disappears way too quickly. The question is where exactly is it going? How is it that you make good money but never seem to have any left at the end of every month? That is the conundrum of the paycheck-to-paycheck lifestyle.

Almost every client I work with has been living paycheck to paycheck to some extent. They've gotten stuck in bad habits and made some mistakes with their money. By the time I see them, they are experiencing feelings of guilt, shame, embarrassment, anger, and sometimes bitterness. They think their situation is impossible and often ask me if there is any hope for them. My answer is always YES, but it may not be easy. Moving ahead is going to require a change in attitude and mindset. As you embark on this journey toward financial freedom, you will probably have to change some of your priorities (at least temporarily). My clients always have a choice about what they're going to do, though, and you have that same choice. You get to decide your time frame and how much or how little you are going to put into this plan. If you refuse to stop spending money on every want, it's going to take you a lot longer to accomplish the goal of breaking the paycheck-to-paycheck cycle, and you may never get out of it. On the other hand, if you allow yourself to think about your Why-What-How and actively pursue this plan, you'll be well on your way to making your financial goals a reality.

Increase Your Financial Awareness

You work really hard for your money. You might even be working a lot of overtime or more than one job trying to take care of your family's needs. So, do you know where your hard-earned money is going? Do you know where you might be overspending? Are you house poor, meaning that your mortgage or rent is taking up a large portion of your net income? Is it credit card debt repayments? Eating out? You might be able to take a pretty good guess, but until you start tracking where your money is going, that's all you have–a guess. And a guess is not good enough. I knew that I was spending a lot on clothes and eating out, but it wasn't until I began keeping track that I realized how much was truly going out to those areas. My guesses fell significantly short of reality!

Let's start this awareness part of the plan by writing down all your information so you have it in front of you on paper and not just in your head. You will find charts for you to complete in the next section. You can peak ahead if you want a preview of what kind of information you will need.

If this is your first time completing charts like these, you will probably have to do some research to figure out how much you typically spend on things like groceries, eating out, and other discretionary expenses. Look at your checkbook, bank statement, and credit card statements for the past three to six months to help you determine your average monthly spending in these categories. For example, if you find that you and your family spent $255 in eating out for Month 1, $184 in Month 2 and $311 in Month 3, you would use an average of $250 (255 + 184 + 311) for that line item.

You might run into trouble coming up with a dollar amount for categories like groceries, pet food and supplies, and household items if you often buy those things at the same store. They will appear on your bank or credit card statement as one lump sum. If you don't have any receipts to review, I recommend thinking in terms of percentages. If you have an amount of $200 that you spent using your debit card, what percentage of that was probably spent for each category given what you think to be true? For me, it would probably be something like 75% on groceries, 10% on pet food, and 15% on household items, which would mean I had spent $150 on groceries, $20 on my cat, and $30 on my household. It's not an exact science. It's just a starting point until you get more information.

Even if you faithfully keep a budget, I want you to look back at your checkbook and statements to determine whether your proposed budget is truly reflecting your spending. What often happens is that you create a budget of where you *want* your money to go, but then you don't record your expenses and go back to see if your spending aligned with the budget that you created for the month. It's kind of like planning for a vacation. You plan ahead for how much you think you'll spend on things like gas, lodging, food, and entertainment. But if you don't keep track of what you actually spent, then you don't know if you went overboard or maybe saved yourself some money.

Remember, you are creating a snapshot, and it may be a little blurry. It's an initial look at what is going on with your money. Later, we will look at how to clean it up. So, go grab your checkbook, bank and credit card statements, and a pencil (you will want to be able to make changes). Then take some time and complete the charts. Hey, don't just look at them . . . write numbers in them! You can also use the blank charts in the back of the book. If you don't like adding numbers yourself, I have included a couple of websites that have spreadsheets which will calculate the numbers for you.

A Word About Irregular Income

If you have an irregular income because you get paid mostly through commissions or because you're self-employed, you're not alone. More people are bringing in this kind of income either as a side hustle or as their full-time career. When recording this type of income on the chart, I suggest looking at the last six to twelve months to see what your two lowest-income months were. Then use the average of these two months. This will give you a conservative estimate so that your budget will work even at your slowest times. You could also use an average from a whole year, especially if your income deviates widely depending on the season. We will talk more about dealing with an irregular income later in the book. For now, we just need a starting point and it should be a conservative number.

Your Snapshot Details

I'm going to walk you through all of the steps of creating a realistic spending plan that works for you. We will explore your monthly net income, monthly expenses including fixed and discretionary expenses, your debt repayment plan, and nonmonthly expenses – those payments that come up quarterly or twice a year. For each section you will calculate the numbers that reflect your *current* situation so that you can prepare to move on to your *ideal* situation. Ready? Let's get started.

Monthly Net Income: Whereas gross income is your total income without any taxes or deductions taken out yet, your net income is basically the amount of your paycheck and what you have available to spend. That's the number we want to work with. If you don't receive a regular paycheck as an employee (i.e., you own a business), then you will need to account for taxes and other deductions before writing in your income. Alternatively, you could include those as fixed expenses on that same-named chart.

Monthly Income #1 is to record *your* net income. Monthly Income #2 is for recording the net income for your spouse or significant other. Other Income could be anything additional that you receive regularly on a monthly basis such as alimony or a second job. It could also include cash payments that you receive for odd jobs, things you sell online, or payments from things like donating plasma or something similar. If you're going to include this kind of income, just make sure you use a conservative number since the income is probably not the same amount every month.

Monthly Income #1:	$
Monthly Income #2:	$
Other Income:	$
Other Income:	$
Total Monthly Net Income:	$

Monthly Expenses: Now it's time to see where all that money is going. You will see in the following chart that the monthly expenses are divided into two categories. Fixed expenses are ones that you usually pay the same amount every month, such as utilities or rent or mortgage – what you might refer to as "your bills". Discretionary expenses are ones that fluctuate and that you have more control over, such as eating out and household items. Notice that I have not included non-monthly expenses or debt repayment like credit cards and school loans in this chart. Those will be recorded in another chart. Also, make sure you do not include health or life insurance expenses if they are already deducted from your paycheck.

You will see that I have included Savings as a fixed expense. It is not a category that most people typically contribute to on a monthly basis, especially when they're living paycheck to paycheck. If the same is true for you, then you're going to put a zero in that space. Now the fact is that you *should* be contributing money to your savings. If you don't have your emergency fund established yet, this is where you will budget for that "expense." When you see the whole picture and get to the part of fine-tuning your plan, you will have the chance to include an amount for the Savings category. As you work on completing these charts, if your eyes start glazing over or you get overwhelmed, take a short break and come back to it. Just make sure you come back!

Fixed Expenses		**Discretionary Expenses**	
Church/Charity	$	Groceries	$
Savings	$	Eating Out	$
Mortgage/Rent	$	Household Items	$
Car Payment 1	$	Personal Hygiene	$
Car Payment 2	$	Kids Expenses	$
Home Phone	$	Babysitting	$
Cell Phone	$	Clothes	$
Electricity	$	Vacation/Travel	$
Water	$	Pet Food/Supplies	$
Gas	$	Entertainment/Hobbies	$
Trash/Recycling	$	Dry Cleaning	$
Cable	$	Subscriptions	$
Internet	$	Memberships	$
Health Insurance	$	Blow Money	$
Life Insurance	$	Miscellaneous	$
Car Insurance	$	Other:	$
Medical	$	Other:	$
Tuition Payment	$		
Other:	$		
Other:	$		
Total Fixed Expenses:	$	Total Discretionary Expenses:	$

Debt Repayments: Debt repayments, although often considered a monthly expense, present challenges and opportunities that the other categories of expenses do not. I am separating them out for a couple of reasons. First, it's important to be aware of how much of your paycheck is going toward minimum debt repayment. Second, we will look at the debt category in-depth in the next chapter and it will be much easier to have this information laid out independently from your other expenses. For this chart, all you are going to include is your minimum monthly payment. We will get into interest rates and balances later. Remember that department store cards *are* credit cards, so those should be included here as well. Note that mortgage and car loan debts are listed in the previous chart under fixed expenses because those are part of your necessary living expenses.

Name of Debt	Minimum Payment
Credit Card #1:	$
Credit Card #2:	$
Credit Card #3:	$
Credit Card #4:	$
Credit Card #5:	$
Credit Card #6:	$
School Loan #1:	$
School Loan #2:	$
School Loan #3:	$
Medical Debt #1:	$
Medical Debt #2:	$
Line of Credit:	$
Personal Loan:	$
Other:	$
Other:	$
Total Debt Payments:	$

Non-Monthly Expenses: These expenses are ones that you might be paying quarterly, semiannually, or annually. Most people tend to forget about these expenses until they get the bill, and then they scramble to pay for them. What you should be doing is including them in your monthly spending plan and saving for them so you have the money when the bill comes due. Let's look at an example to see how to determine how much you should be saving every month for these kinds of expenses.

Let's say that you pay for your car insurance every six months and your payment is $450. To get the monthly payment – how much you should be saving each month – you would divide $450 by 6, which would be $75. In the chart, you would write $450 under Amt Due, 6 under # Months, and $75 under Mo. Pymt.

Expense	Amt Due	# Months	Mo. Pymt
Car Repairs			
Auto Insurance (non-monthly plan)			
Tuition Payment (non-monthly plan)			
Homeowners Insurance			
Property Taxes			
Holiday Expenses			
Other:			
Total Non-Monthly Expenses:			$

The Final Balance. Great job! You now know how much money you have coming in, how much is going out, and where it is going. Now, let's put it together and see what you've got. We're going to go category by category, subtracting each expense category from your total net income. Let's see how much money you potentially are short or have left over at the end of the month.

If you're beginning to feel the anxiety rising, take a deep breath. It's okay. Remember, no shame or embarrassment here. This is just about creating awareness so you can move forward.

You will find the numbers to fill in the blanks by looking for the bolded lines at the bottom of each chart from the previous pages.

Total Monthly Net Income:	$________
Less Total Fixed Expenses:	$________
Balance (subtract #2 from #1):	$________
Less Total Discretionary Expenses:	$________
Balance (subtract #4 from #3):	$________
Less Total Debt Repayments:	$________
Balance (subtract #6 from #5):	$________
Less Total Non-Monthly Expenses:	$________
Final Balance (subtract #8 from #7):	$________

If you ended up with a positive number for your final balance, then your income is enough to cover your expenses, and you have some extra cash flow available every month. Congratulations! If you have a negative number, your expenses are more than your current income and probably the reason that you keep running out of money every month. Either way, stay with me as we look at how to use this information to get you out of the paycheck-to-paycheck trap.

This was just a snapshot, and if it's the first time you have done this kind of exercise or it's been a while, then those discretionary expenses might not be totally accurate yet.

So, let me ask you a question that I asked you earlier. What do you think is keeping you stuck living paycheck to paycheck? Are you overspending in one or more categories? Or do you think you're underearning (not bringing in enough income)? It may be a combination of both. Even if there have been some expenses that were out of your control (e.g., medical debt), have there been other areas that you do have control over that played a factor?

When I'm helping people figure out how to increase their cash flow so they have a positive number as their final balance, I tell them that there are two ways to do this. You either have to spend less or earn more (or more often than not, do both). The majority of them acknowledge that it's a spending issue, at least partly, but in order to get on the right track they also may need to earn more, at least temporarily.

If you haven't figured it out yet, this money snapshot is also a starter budget (I've been using the term spending plan)! After you've done the initial snapshot, then it's time to go back and tweak some of the numbers to come up with a working plan for the month. You will do this shortly.

Zero-Based Budgeting

You may have heard the term zero-based budgeting. It happens when your final balance number comes out to zero. It means that you have assigned every dollar a duty or a role. This is the ultimate budget goal. You do not want money left over in your monthly budget without a place to go or it will disappear. You're familiar with disappearing money, right? So, when you are creating your plan, tweak the numbers so that you end with zero. If you are ending in the negative, you need to bring in more income or cut spending. If you are ending in the positive, you need to send more money to one or more categories, preferably savings or debt repayment. If you have enough money for your emergency account and don't have debt repayments, you can send leftover money to one of your savings buckets which we'll talk about in a later chapter.

Create Your Monthly Plan

Look back at your final balance. If your final balance was a negative number, then you will want to re-evaluate your situation. You need to find a way to either bring in more income or cut some expenses, because your goal is to be at zero. If your final balance was positive, then you still need to figure out where to send the extra money. We will continue to fine-tune this budget in the next chapter, but for right now let's just get to a zero-based budget.

1. Go back to the charts that you completed in this chapter, especially the Expenses chart. Where can you lower some of your expenses? Food? Clothing? Entertainment?
2. You can cross out and write in new numbers on the page or use one of the blank charts in the back of the book.
3. Re-calculate your numbers and continue to re-calculate until you end up with a final balance of zero. You will do this same process every month. If you don't want to add up the numbers yourself, there are several online spreadsheets that you can use that will calculate the numbers for you.

In the next chapter, you will read about one of the most important steps you can take to move beyond the paycheck-to-paycheck lifestyle. I mentioned it earlier. Can you remember what it is?

Spiritual Perspective

Does the Bible talk about budgeting? You bet it does. Although, you probably won't find the actual word *budget*. Instead, we read stories and parables that imply the same principles. Think about a budget or spending plan as a proactive way to *manage* your money. In religious circles, we often use the word *stewardship*. In the Bible, a steward is someone who is the *manager* of property, money, and family for their employer. Today, we translate that to each of us being stewards (managers) of our own property, money, and family.

Joseph is a great example of being a good manager of the resources he was given. In Genesis 41:41-57, we read how he collected food and grain and stored huge amounts of them in the cities of Egypt. When the famine came seven years later (as predicted in Pharaoh's dreams), Egypt was the only place to go to buy grain and other food. This was because of Joseph's (a) obedience to God and (b) diligent planning and acknowledgment that abundance would not last forever. Budgeting is essentially creating a plan, which is exactly what Joseph did.

Luke 12:48 says ". . . From everyone who has been given much, much will be demanded; and from the one who has been entrusted with much, much more will be asked." Although this verse is not specifically addressing money, it is reminding us of our responsibility to use what we have been provided wisely, and that most definitely includes our money.

I challenge you to put a stake in the ground today and begin honoring God with your money decisions. We do not truly own what we have, and it can be taken away from us at any time. You know emergencies are going to happen. Make a plan for your money and be a good steward. Call upon your inner Joseph!

Planning Your Escape

1. What thoughts and feelings came up as you completed the charts? Did you get overwhelmed, anxious, or relieved? Were you thinking about how much you hate tracking money, or were you glad to finally see some real numbers on paper?

2. If you need to increase your income, what options will you try? Look back at the list of ways to do this in the previous chapter to generate ideas.

3. If you have a positive final balance, where will you send your extra money?

4. Creating a budget that works takes time and practice. You will make mistakes. You will slip up and not stick to one of your categories. It's okay. Think back to those scripts you flipped. Are you noticing any of those mindsets coming back in to play as you try to budget? What is holding you back from being able to create a workable spending plan? What tape is running through your head that you need to flip (maybe again)?

CHAPTER 14

Get Out of the Well

Imagine you're driving to work one day just like any other day. You're focused on all of the things that you need to get done, maybe listening to the radio a little bit. You notice the car in front of you has a taillight out. You see a french fry on the floor in the front of the passenger seat. Then, you blink and all of a sudden you realize you're turning into the parking lot. And you think, "Wait. . . how did I get here? Where did that car in front of me go? Last thing I remember, I . . . What was I doing?"

Has that ever happened to you? It's like you were in some kind of fog or trance that made you completely lose track of time. You remember getting in the car and a couple of things along the way and then you blinked and you were at your destination. Kind of scary, isn't it?

Getting into debt often happens in a similar way. You start out knowing that you owe a little bit of money and then one day you realize that little bit has grown into a mountain. And you wonder, "How did that happen? The last thing I remember . . . How did it grow to be so much?" The fear begins to choke you and you can hardly breathe. What are you going to do?

Most people believe that having debt is normal and just part of everyday life. I used to think that way too. Everyone I knew had some kind of debt, whether it be credit cards, a car loan, a school loan, or a mortgage. Think about it. How many people do you personally know who do *not* have at least one debt payment? Anyone? Those people are few in number but slowly gaining ground. People are tired of losing money and watching it go to someone else. Getting into debt is incredibly easy. It often occurs after an extended time of not paying attention to how much you've been spending. It happens when you buy more house than you can afford. It happens when you buy a more luxurious car than you need. And it occurs when you're hit with a major crisis.

Some think about debt as primarily credit cards and maybe school loans. They don't give mortgage, car loan, and medical debt the same weight. I think it might be because credit cards and school loans get the most media attention; credit cards because they are "bad" and school loans because they are so astronomically high right now. But they all fit the definition of debt, which, in the simplest terms, is owing money to someone, whether it's a bank, a credit card company, or your grandmother who gave you a loan. It's borrowing money with the intent to pay it back at a later date. It's an easy way to get what we want *now* without having to save first.

So, is having debt really that bad? After all, some debt is good, right? Like school loans, a mortgage, and money borrowed to start a business. Here's what I think. When you owe money to someone else, no matter what the reason, you are financially tied to that person or organization. You are a borrower, not an owner. There's a big difference between the two. I hate owing money. I've been there and done that more times than I can count. It's stressful and exhausting and not the way I want to live. And not the way I want you to live either. It's time to climb out of the well. It's time to take action.

Step 3: Pay Off That Debt

Your mission, should you choose to accept it, is to be an "owner" of everything you have, instead of a borrower.

Although many families say they don't want to be in debt (and I believe they are sincere), they struggle to break free from it. They continue to rack up more and stay stuck. How many times have you decided to "become debt-free"? When was the last time you made a resolution to stop spending money and start paying off those credit cards? What keeps getting in your way of following through on this dream? How often do you think, "Sure, it would be nice to be debt-free, but it's totally unrealistic." Or "I will always have a monthly debt payment; there's no way around it." Here's my response: no, it's not unrealistic and no, you don't always have to have a monthly payment. But you've got to start *now*. Don't put this off any longer, because it's not going away (unless you decide to declare bankruptcy, which we'll talk about a little later).

I get that paying off large amounts of debt seems like it will take forever and there are a lot of other things you would like to spend your money on. Life is short and you want to have fun and have nice things. It's relatively easy to just pay the monthly minimum and use any extra cash flow for things that give you immediate satisfaction. I get it. Really, I do. When faced with these motivation challenges, I go back to a couple of questions: (1) how would it feel to not have the weight and stress of all that debt every day, and (2) what would you be able to do with all that extra money if you didn't have to pay those particular expenses every month?

Let's say you're beginning to see things my way and are at least considering the idea of paying off all your debts (aside from the mortgage for now). One of the fastest ways to create long-term extra cash flow is by paying off your debt and staying out of it. But, where do you start? The first step is to create that awareness you read about earlier. If you've been ignoring your debt and have no idea what your balances are or the minimum payments or interest rates, it's time to become acquainted with them again. Look again at your Total Debt Payment amount from the previous chapter (if you skipped over it, it's okay but I need you to go back and do it now). Write your Total Debt Payments number from the last line here: $______________.

I know this number may make you sick to your stomach and feel all kinds of fear, guilt, and shame. Take a deep breath and embrace those feelings. Cry if you need to. Blame whoever you need to blame. Okay, now let's start moving forward and take control of the debt and start changing your financial future. Ready?

Debt Snowball vs. Debt Avalanche

I am often asked how to decide which debt to pay off first. Should you pay off debt with the lowest balance or the highest interest rate? The vast majority of the time, I say pay off the debt with the lowest balance. By quickly paying off one of your debts, you will likely get an emotional boost, which leads to the motivation to start working on the next one.

To get all of your debt eliminated in the fastest time possible, you need to go beyond making the minimum payments. Continuing to pay the minimum amount (which probably includes a lot of interest) *will* take you what feels like forever.

Paying off debt from lowest to highest balance is part of a process called the debt snowball. You may have heard of it, as it gets a lot of attention when discussing debt reduction and elimination. One of the definitions of *snowball* is "to increase rapidly in size, intensity, or importance." With regard to debt, you are trying to increase the intensity of paying it off. The more money you can throw at it, the faster it goes down.

Here are the steps for a successful debt snowball:

1. List all of your debts (except your mortgage) from smallest to largest.
2. Pay the minimum amount due on all of your debt repayments.
3. Determine how much extra money you can add to your minimum monthly payment with the lowest balance to get it paid off faster.
4. Once that balance is paid off, take the amount you've been paying toward that debt and put it all toward the next lowest debt.

5. Keep working this process of taking the payment that you were making on the lower balance and rolling it into the next higher balance until all of your debt is paid off. This is the snowball.
6. Be patient and persistent. This could take several years if you have a lot of debt and don't have a lot of money to put into the snowball. The beauty of the snowball happens when you are able to pay a significant amount of extra cash to that lowest balance and accelerate the payoff.

If you insist that paying off the higher interest rate debt is more beneficial to your financial plan, then you will be following what is sometimes called the *debt avalanche.* It is very similar to the debt snowball but you accelerate the debt with the highest interest rate instead of the lowest balance. Although this approach might initially seem like the best way to go because you think you'll be saving money in interest, it's not necessarily the best way to achieve your goal of being debt-free. It's true that you may save some in interest, but you also might get more frustrated and give up because it takes longer to get each debt paid off, especially the first one.

Ultimately, you've got to do what fits your debt repayment personality better. Some people just can't get their head wrapped around paying off the lowest balance and are focused on the interest rate. If that's the case for you, then you might be more successful using the debt avalanche method. However, if you are like me (and most others), you are motivated by fast progress and the emotional high it gives. I recommend you at least try the snowball method first and see how it works.

Debt Management Companies

Should you work with a debt management company or some other organization that says they will manage your debt for you? I would be very careful about this and do diligent research before agreeing to anything. These companies can work on your behalf to talk with creditors and reduce monthly payments and/or interest rates. You pay the company a monthly fee and then they pay your creditors. It sounds like a great plan. But there are a couple of things you need to consider. First, you are no longer in control of your debt repayments. Second, there can be a lot of different fees involved, which cut into your savings.

This kind of program has worked for a few people that I know but you can essentially do the same thing as these companies by calling your creditors and talking with them yourself. Learning how to manage your own debt is an important step in staying away from it in the future, because you will have hands-on experience as to how hard it was to get out. Plus, *you* want to be able to control the time table and the amount that is going toward the debt repayment. Finally, the pride that you will feel when you have taken control and done it on your own is undeniable.

Declaring Bankruptcy

Another question I'm often asked is, Should I declare bankruptcy? This depends on your current situation, but it should most certainly be a last resort. I know it can sound like a quick way to erase a lot of stress. But you need to consider the potential consequences as well. Filing bankruptcy can hurt your credit score and be on your credit report for several years. Depending on the type of bankruptcy that you file for, there is also the possibility for loss of property and possessions.

If you got yourself into the debt well you're in by overspending and buying more than you could afford, then take responsibility and create your plan to get out of it. Declaring bankruptcy won't fix the behaviors that got you to this point.

It's possible that you have debt due to a situation that was out of your control. For example, medical debt is not something that you choose to accumulate, and it can cripple a family dealing with severe medical issues. Insurance usually only covers so much, and you're still responsible for the deductible, co-pays, possibly some medical equipment, and other bills. This might be a case for filing bankruptcy but again, as a very last resort.

Keep in mind that there are certain types of debt, such as school loans, child support, and taxes which cannot be discharged through bankruptcy.

Interest: What You Need to Know

One last important area I want to discuss is interest. When you have debt, interest is working *against* you. It is what can make a manageable hill become an unmovable mountain very quickly. Have you looked at how much you are paying every month in total interest payments? Have you ever looked at how much you have paid in interest over the past year? That was one of the key motivators that made me get focused on paying off my debt. I realized that I was spending hundreds of dollars in interest (oh, and late fees too!). I kept thinking about what I could do with that extra money.

In contrast, when you have money in savings and investments, interest is working *for* you. Instead of feeling stressed at how much more money is going out, you get excited about how much money is coming in. That's called *passive income* and it's a lot of fun to watch your accounts grow without having to do anything. And of course, the more money you have in your account, the more interest you gain. Even more exciting is the idea of compound interest which is interest added to your interest, which makes your money grow even faster! We'll talk more about this when we talk about investments in Chapter 15.

Your Debt Elimination Plan

Now, let's put what you learned into practice and create a plan to pay off that debt.

The first step is to get organized so we can set the debt snowball in motion. We are going to list all our debt and the minimum monthly payments, just as we did in the Debt Chart in the previous chapter. But this time we will add the current balances and the interest rates. We are also going to list them in order from lowest balance to highest balance. This is the order in which we will pay them off – the start of the snowball process.

Note that this plan takes into account the fact that you are current with your debts and paying the minimum monthly amounts on time (not incurring late fees). If you have debt in collections, they should not be part of your debt snowball yet. Once you have taken care of your current debt, you can go back and work with defaulted debt and the collection agencies.

A word of warning – please be careful about making a payment to a debt that you have not paid on in a while or is in collections. Doing so can cause you more problems down the road if you don't do it the right way. I recommend you talk with a financial coach or financial advisor about your options.

Here is an example of a Debt Chart for you to look at before you do your own chart at the end of the chapter. To simplify things, I have not included payments and interest rates for the line of credit and school loans. However, if you have those, make sure you include them on your chart.

Name of Debt	Balance	Min. Payment	Interest Rate
Credit Card #1: Dept Store 1	$234.00	$15.00	21.99%
Credit Card #2: ABC Visa	$1,250.00	$25.00	12.99%
Medical Debt #1: Hospital	$1,500.00	n/a	n/a
Other: loan from dad	$2,000.00	n/a	n/a
Credit Card #3: Dept Store 2	$3,642.00	$45.00	24.99%
Credit Card #4: Mastercard	$5,200.00	$55.00	0%
Line of Credit: House Maintenance	$10,350.00		
School Loan #1: Federal (Hers)	$12,000.00		
School Loan #2: Private (Hers)	$20,000.00		
School Loan #3: Private (His)	$35,000.00		
Total Debt:	**$91,176**	—	—

Now, that we have it all written down in an organized format, we're ready for the next step. We need to decide on an extra monthly amount that we're going to add to the minimum payment of that lowest debt. Looking at this example, the lowest balance is a credit card for $234 and the minimum amount due every month is $15. Let's say we look at our budget and see that if we brought our lunch to work instead of eating out once each week, we would have an additional $50 that we can add to debt repayment. This means that instead of paying $15 every month, we would be paying $65 every month. Can you see how much more quickly that balance of $234 would be paid off if you were paying $65 instead of $15? Let me show you. If you stayed with the minimum $15, it would take you 19 months to pay that card off (and you would pay $44 in interest). By paying the extra $50 per month (total of $65), you would have the balance paid off in less than 4 months (and only pay about $10 in interest)! Nineteen months or four months? I'll take the latter, thank you very much!

With that debt taken care of (yay!), it's time to focus on the next one, which is the second credit card debt of $1,250. This card has a minimum monthly payment of $25. We've still been paying that $25 every month but now we are going to take the $65 that we were applying to the first credit card debt and add it to this second one. So, instead of paying $25 per month, we will be paying $90. What happens with the payoff timeline now? We go from 73 months – yes, that's just over six years – to 16 months, or a little over a year! And we save almost $450 in interest! Do you see how powerful this is? That's the snowball effect in action.

You'll notice that there is no minimum payment or interest rate on the medical debt or the loan from dad. This often happens with these kinds of debt. Many times, you will get a date that it must be paid by and if it's not paid, you will incur late fees. You can also usually request to set up a monthly payment plan. When we have paid off credit card #2 in our example, we would have $90 per month to put toward the medical debt. We would then talk with the creditor to establish a payment plan based on this amount.

You continue to do this with each debt rolling the monthly payment amount from the previous debt to the current minimum on the next one.

Now, what if we were able to contribute an extra $75 or $100 per month? What if you used birthday or Christmas money or bonus money from your job to throw at the debt? How do you think that would change the timeline for getting debt free? You're right. You would get debt-free even faster.

Now it's your turn to complete step 3. You'll find a blank chart to use in the Planning Your Escape activity section. Then, in the next chapter, we're going to talk about something a lot more fun, and it's much easier to do once this step is taken care of!

This is not an easy step. It's requires you to make some tough choices. People often want to continue spending on luxury items, such as vacations, clothes, and household projects while they're trying to get out of debt. They want to continue spending a lot of money on birthday and Christmas presents. Here's the thing – there will *always* be something you can spend money on. I know that sometimes there are emergencies that you will need to spend money on. And there will be other kinds of unexpected expenses. However, luxury items, like those mentioned a minute ago, are not an emergency. Christmas and birthdays are going to come every year – plan for them by setting aside a fixed amount every month. It's your choice. What are you going to do?

Spiritual Perspective

I had always believed that it was a sin to have debt. Later, I learned that belief is actually not biblical. There is not a single verse in the Bible that I'm aware of that says having debt is a sin. Good to know, right? But if that's true, why are we taught that we shouldn't carry debt and why do we feel so guilty about having it? Well, it may not be a sin, but the Bible does warn us about the dangers of having debt and it reminds us to be content in what we do have. You may be familiar with these passages:

- "But godliness with contentment is great gain. For we brought nothing into the world and we can take nothing out of it. But if we have food and clothing, we will be content with that." (1 Timothy 6:6-8)
- "The rich rule over the poor, and the borrower is slave to the lender." (Proverbs 22:7)
- "The wicked borrow and do not repay, but the righteous give generously." (Psalm 37:21)

Being in debt prevents you from being able to:

- Bless a family member, neighbor, or friend in need.
- Tithe to your home church
- Be physically and emotionally healthy
- Save for retirement
- Give generously

Planning Your Escape

Now, it's your turn to complete the Debt Chart with your own numbers. You can refer to the Debt Chart that you did in the previous chapter to find the name of the debt and minimum payment. This time, however, you're going to include the current balance and interest rate. I also want you to list your debts from their lowest balance to the highest balance. This is the order you will pay off each debt.

Name of Debt	Balance	Min. Payment	Interest Rate
Total Debt:		—	—

Great job! Now, that you have it all written down in an organized format, you're ready for the next step. You need to decide on an extra monthly amount that you are going to add to your minimum payment of that lowest debt so you can get it paid off quicker. Go back to your spending plan if you need help figuring out what that amount is going to be.

Write the extra monthly amount that you are going to add to snowball your debt: $___________

What date would you like to have all your debt paid off? You can just write the number of months or years if that is easier to think about. Go ahead and write that date here: ____________________

Note: I have included a couple debt snowball resources in the back of the book. Using one of these online resources will allow you to input your information and automatically calculate the snowball process for you.

CHAPTER 15

Supersize your Savings

You made it through the first half of the plan, which entailed a lot of organizing, prioritizing, and probably making some tough decisions. Now we look at the last three steps of the six-step plan. I refer to steps 4, 5, and 6 as supersizing your savings, because when taken together, that's exactly what you'll do. Once you finish your debt snowball, you'll be able to use the money you've been paying toward eliminating debt for a focused plan of staying *out* of debt for good.

This savings chapter is crucial to your escape from the paycheck-to-paycheck trap. I know that after paying off all that debt, you're excited to finally have extra cash flow available. And it will be very tempting to go on a spending spree and purchase some things that you have been putting off. I urge you to hold off on that for a little longer. You need to save some more money first. Having this level of savings will not only prevent you from going into debt again but will give you a sense of peace and security. So, let's go through each step one at a time.

Step 4: Save a Minimum of 3–6 Months' Expenses

It's not nearly enough to have $1,000 in an emergency fund. That is just to get you started and help with minor crises that come along while you work on paying off your debt. Once you are debt-free other than your mortgage, it's time to up the ante, so you have money for more expensive emergencies or in case you have a reduction or loss of income (that's your Why). It is widely recommended that you have three to six months of necessary expenses saved. I tend to be more conservative, so I usually recommend the higher end of the range. If you are single, only one spouse works, or the majority of the income comes from a business, I would recommend having closer to six to eight months in this fund.

This fund is for *emergencies* just like the initial fund was. You shouldn't withdraw money from it unless absolutely necessary. And you've already determined what constitutes an emergency, right? I know this step will feel overwhelming when you look at the amount of money that I'm telling you to save. Remember that money that you were sending to your debt snowball every month? Now it's time to apply it to this extended emergency fund. It might take several months – maybe even more than a year or two – to get this amount saved. But be patient. Think about how you will feel to have this kind of money saved up and you won't have to worry about how you're going to have to pay for an unexpected emergency.

How much do you really need? How do you determine how much money you actually need to have accumulated in this emergency fund? Look back at your budget and Expense chart. The money that you need to accumulate for this step depends on your monthly *fixed expenses*. It will include a couple of your discretionary expenses, such as groceries and some personal hygiene items, but for the most part, you are looking at necessary expenses that must be paid every month. You can live without cable television, eating out, and other luxury items.

You will add up those fixed and necessary expenses and then multiply by the number of months you have decided to have your fund based upon – minimum of three months. Remember, you should use the money that you had been contributing to your debt snowball to fund this account. For example, if you spend $5,000 per month on necessary expenses, the goal is to accumulate a minimum of $15,000 in this three-month extended emergency fund. I know this sounds daunting. Take it step by step and you'll get there. If you want to fast-track this step, find a way to cut some expenses or bring in some extra income using the same process that we talked about in creating your initial emergency fund and getting out of debt.

You may be wondering what to do when you need to pay for something that isn't an emergency. You want to replace your old dishwasher, your car is beginning to cost more than it's worth, you need a new roof, or you want to be able to take a nice family vacation. Where does that fit in? Great question, and we'll look at that coming up in the step 6.

Step 5: Invest 15% of Your Income

Are you ready to start supersizing your savings so you are prepared for almost anything that comes along? This is where we start! In this section, we will focus on investments and retirement planning. If you remember back in Chapter 8, I recommended you allocate 10% of your income to investing. That is a minimum. The goal is to invest at *least 15%* to this category. If you are behind in your retirement savings, once you get your debt paid off and your extended emergency fund completed, you may want to contribute even more to play catch-up.

I am a financial coach, not a financial advisor, so I am not going to give you specific investing advice. What I *can* do is share some basic ways to get started so you can ramp it up and *really* supersize your savings. Once you're ready to dive into the world of investing, start doing some research of your own and learn more about your options.

So, what should you do to get started investing? Here are some steps I recommend:

1. First, you need to **get out of debt** (except your mortgage, if you have one). There are differing opinions on this, but I tend to side with the belief that extra cash flow should be directed to obtaining your three to six months of emergency fund savings and then paying down your debt before investing.
2. **Get familiar with all the terminology** in the investment world. For example, understand the difference between a Roth IRA account and a traditional IRA, 401(k), 403(b), TSP; stocks vs. bonds, and simple vs. compound interest, and growth fund vs. value fund.
3. If you are not contributing to your workplace retirement

account, **do it!** The matching programs that many employers offer is *free money* that you shouldn't pass up. If your company matches what you put in (usually up to a certain percentage or dollar amount), contribute as much as you can to take full advantage of the match. There are usually HR representatives who can help you decide how to invest. Just be sure you do your own research and don't simply take their word for it.

4. If you have one or more retirement accounts already, **review your last statements** to see what you are invested in. Most people have no idea what kind of funds they are in, how those funds are doing, or even what their balances are. It's time to look at them now. If the statement looks like a foreign language to you, talk to someone that can help you with it. *Look at your fees and expense ratios.* The more fees you have and the higher your expense ratios (i.e., over 1.0) the less money you will make.
5. **Sign up for a Roth IRA.** As of this writing in 2019, you can contribute $6,000 annually and after age fifty, you can contribute $7,000. With a Roth account, you pay taxes now, before you invest, and you withdraw it tax-free later. There are income limits, however, when it comes to contributing to a Roth account. For single filers, if your Modified Adjusted Gross Income is over $122,000, your contributed is limited, and if it's over $137,000, you're ineligible to contribute to a Roth. If you're married filing jointly, the contribution is limited beginning at $193,000 and ineligible at $203,000. Contributing to a Roth IRA is separate from contributing to a 401(k) or 403(b) plan; you want to be able to do both if possible. If you don't have access to a retirement plan at

work, the Roth IRA is your next best investment if you meet the income requirements. You can learn more about these accounts at https://www.rothira.com.

6. **Balance your investments.** If you invest 100% of your money in your company stock or international funds or bonds or aggressive growth funds and that's all you're invested in, that's a huge risk. Any one of those funds could tank at some point, but it is much less likely that all of them will at the same time. I agree with the predominant belief that you should have a mix of funds. If you're new to investing an easy way to do this is to invest in what is called a balanced fund because . . . it's already balanced.
7. If you are self-employed you can still have access to a retirement plan. It's called a **Simplified Employee Pension (SEP).** It is very similar to a traditional IRA plan.
8. **Don't invest in something you don't understand.** This is where you really can lose money. Find a financial advisor to help you with your investing decisions. If you don't know where to go, ask your family, friends, and coworkers who they use and then interview a couple of advisors to see who you feel comfortable with. If you're married, *both* of you should feel comfortable with that person. Ask questions and do your research. Be careful not to read or listen to just one source. Just because you've read about a certain investment fund being a great opportunity, it doesn't mean it's right for you.
9. **Be patient and let time work for you.** When stocks are up, we get excited because we see our accounts grow. But when stocks are down and we see our portfolio drop, it can make us want to get out. If you know that your investments have

a good track record, hang in there. You don't need to check your account balance every week or even every month. A six-month or annual review is enough for most people.

10. **Get excited about compound interest!** There is a reason that Albert Einstein called compound interest the "eighth wonder of the world" and said "He who understands it, earns it... He who doesn't... pays it." Remember how we talked about interest being a huge negative when trying to pay off your debt? Well, the opposite is true when it comes to your investments. Interest is what makes your investments grow. Compound interest makes it grow more rapidly.

There is *so* much more to investing that I have not discussed here, but that is not the purpose of this book. Check out the Resources section for a couple of books that have detailed information about this topic. The more informed you are, the better decisions you will be able to make about your financial future. As I mentioned earlier, a financial advisor should be a part of your team in helping you to make your decisions. An advisor will talk with you about your "investing personality," future financial goals, and help you come up with a plan on where to invest your hard-earned money.

Investing a portion of your money is critical to your financial success. Don't let lack of knowledge, fear, or intimidation keep you from completing this step.

Step 6: Create Additional Savings Buckets and Pay Off Your Mortgage

I talked about savings buckets earlier in the book. What are they? This is where you put the money you are saving for semiannual or annual expense such as car insurance, expenses that will be coming down the road such as replacing a home improvement project, and luxuries such as a vacation. They can't easily be put into your budget as a one-time expense. To establish a savings bucket, first determine how much what you want is going to cost. Then figure out when you want to have the money by. Based on that you can determine how much you need to save each month. Last step: start saving for it!

For example, let's say you want to take a family vacation in the next six months. You estimate that it will cost $3,000, which includes hotel, travel, food, and fun. You take that $3,000 and divide by 6 months to determine you need to save $500 per month. If you can't afford that much per month, then you either need to wait longer to take the vacation, find a way to lower the expenses, or bring in some extra money for a while.

I know this may not be the way you've done things before. You've probably just put what you wanted on a credit card and then figured out how to pay for it later. But that's what landed you in debt and living paycheck to paycheck. It's time to start thinking ahead. I kept my sofa and loveseat for nineteen years. It had rips in the leather cushions, stretch marks, and cat claws on the ends. There were several other things that I wanted in that time as well, including a new television and some landscaping projects. I created savings buckets for them and steadily put money into them every month. I recently got a great Black Friday deal on my new furniture, paid for with cash.

So, think about the large purchases you want to make and get ready to make a bucket for each one. I recommend you give these buckets simple names like "vacation fund," "car fund," "house account," "furniture fund," or "vet fund." Then begin allocating your resources.

You have a few choices for where you can keep these various funds:

- **Multiple savings accounts at your bank or credit union.** Find out if your bank will allow you to have more than one savings account at no cost. This is the ideal way to handle these funds. For example, I have one for vacation, one for car, and one for household, which includes homeowner's insurance and property taxes. With many employers and banks, you can have a specific amount directly deposited from your paycheck into each account. That makes it easy to stay organized. Plus, you're less likely to spend it when you don't have access to it right away.
- **One savings account, separate from your emergency fund.** This setup is okay to do, but you will likely find it is more difficult to keep track of how much you have in each bucket. You will need to keep good records at home. Again, have an amount direct deposited into the account if possible.
- **Jars or envelopes at home.** I don't recommend this if you feel too tempted to "borrow" from them or if you're uncomfortable having too much cash in your house.
- **A combination of the above.** The point here is flexibility. Try different options and do what works best for you.

What about saving for children's college tuition? I'm glad you asked! I like to think of this expense as another bucket, a very large bucket. You should start saving for your children's college tuition as early as possible, but *not* before you have finished step four, where you have paid off debt and have your full emergency fund in place. Many states offer a 529 plan or something similar, which is a tax-advantaged savings plan designed for future education costs. All plans are not equal, so you will want to do some homework to determine which one is right for you if you decide to go this route. You can talk with your financial advisor or bank representative about the best way to save up for this expense.

Pay off your mortgage

Once you have some savings buckets established, it's time to turn your attention to your mortgage (if you have one). Paying off your mortgage is essentially your last step to becoming debt-free and moving toward financial freedom! If your mortgage is for thirty years, take a look at refinancing for fifteen years. Although many choose to refinance in order to use the equity to pay for some kind of large expense like a home improvement project, I want you to look at it as a stepping stone to becoming debt-free. This may increase your monthly payment, but it will shave off a lot of interest. The interest is nearly all you're paying for in the beginning of your loan. Refinancing is not for everyone and deciding whether it makes sense for you can be a little complex. I'm not an expert in this area, so I encourage you to do your own research and talk with a realtor and someone from your bank before making this decision. That said, here are a couple of things to consider when determining if you should refinance.

- If you are not planning to stay in your house for more than a few years or if you don't have too many years of the loan remaining, refinancing may not be a good option. It takes time to break even and for the savings to actually work for you. There are online calculators that you can use to calculate your break-even point to see if refinancing makes sense for your situation.
- Look for a new mortgage loan with a lower fixed interest rate. This will help you save even more money in the long-term. I do not recommend getting an adjustable- rate mortgage

(ARM) or any kind of variable-rate mortgage because you want your payments to be the same amount every month.
- It is critical that you have money saved up to pay for the fees and closing costs. You can talk with your realtor or bank representative or use an online calculator to get an idea of what these costs might be for your situation.
- Make sure there are no prepayment penalties if you want to pay the mortgage off early. Don't make an assumption about this. Make sure you have it in writing.

If you plan to stay in your house for several years or more, I recommend paying the mortgage off as soon as possible. This is one of the smartest things I ever did.

The process for paying off my mortgage began by refinancing from a thirty-year loan to a fifteen-year loan and dropping from a 7.5% interest rate to a 5.5% interest rate. Then, a couple of years later, I started contributing extra money almost every month, making sure that my additional money was applied to the *principal* balance, not interest. This is important because it is the principal amount that you are trying to pay off which will in turn decrease the interest amount. I wrote on the memo line of the check: Extra $200 (or whatever the amount was) for Principal only. Some banks automatically apply additional money to principal. Check with your bank and see what their policy is. If you make your mortgage payment online as many do now, it may be easier to designate that extra payment.

If you want to pay off your mortgage early, here are a couple of ways for you to do that:

- Pay your mortgage payment biweekly. By making twenty-six half-payments, you end up making thirteen full payments instead of twelve each year thus lowering your principal balance and interest. You will want to make sure your mortgage allows you to do this. A word of caution: avoid paying your bank or a third-party company to do this process for you. You can accomplish it on your own.

- Pay an additional lump sum every month to the principal balance. After you've filled a couple of your priority savings buckets, you can then start applying some of that extra money toward paying off your mortgage. You can also go back to your budget and see where there is money available to direct toward this process.

Just think about what you would be able to do if you didn't have to make the mortgage payment every month! Having that extra money available exponentially increased my ability to supersize my savings.

When you have completed these six steps, you will discover you have, at long last, escaped the paycheck-to-paycheck trap, and you will be on your way to finding financial freedom on the other side. You will start to feel confidence, peace, and security even as you begin step one, and those feelings will continue to grow as you move through each step.

Your entire plan can go way off course, however, when a crisis occurs out of the blue, especially if it's a big one. Is there a way to prepare and protect yourself from that? As a matter of fact, yes there is, and we're going to talk about it in the next chapter.

Spiritual Perspective

Does saving money mean that you don't trust God to provide for you and your family? No. On the contrary, planning and saving is something that we are instructed to do. Take these two verses for example:

- "The wise store up choice food and olive oil, but fools gulp theirs down." (Proverbs 21:20)
- "A wise man thinks ahead; a fool doesn't, and even brags about it." (Proverbs 13:16, TLB)

In other words, we are smart to put money aside for the future and foolish to spend it all. In *Smart Woman's Guide to Retirement Planning*, Mary Hunt cautions her readers about following the "Faith-Based Retirement Plan,"[8] in which people tend to "have faith that everything will work out." I had to smile when I read it because it sounded like what I have heard so many Christians say when they are in the middle of a crisis. I've even said it myself. And it's often true. Here's the thing – God will absolutely provide for us, but He will not always rescue us from our poor choices like excessive spending and getting into debt.

I do want to mention a word of caution about supersizing your savings: we need to be careful that we do not end up hoarding our money out of fear of the unknown or a desire to become rich. We are always called to put our hope and trust in God. A desire to be wealthy is not bad if we use that wealth to take care of our family and bless others. We are not meant to keep it all for ourselves.

Planning Your Escape

1. What savings buckets do you want to create?

2. Where are you going to keep your savings buckets?

3. How much do you need to save and how much will you put in each bucket each month to reach that goal?

4. What step do you need to take with your investment plan? Check all that apply and write a date as to when you will get this activity completed.

___ I need to review my statement to see what I'm invested in and what my fees are.
Date: ______________________________

___ I need to talk to my employer about my retirement plan and investment options.
Date: ______________________________

___ I need to start contributing to my workplace retirement plan, a Roth IRA, or another plan outside of my workplace.
Date: ______________________________

___ I need to research the various investment terms, so I can make informed decisions about my investment portfolio.
Date: ______________________________

___ I need to make an appointment with a financial coach or a financial advisor.
Date: ______________________________

5. If you have a mortgage, when would you like to have it paid off by? How much extra per month would you need to pay toward principal to accomplish this goal?

PART III

Stay Out of the Trap

CHAPTER 16

Curveballs and Crises

I will never forget May of 1978. I was eleven years old, and my cousin, Trudy, and I were waiting for our parents to pick us up from an after-school Girl Scouts meeting. To my surprise, when my uncle showed up, he said that I was going home with them. Cool! But my uncle was very quiet and didn't seem like he was in a very good mood. So, my cousin and I just sat quietly, with her in the front and me in the back seat of the car, for the less than two-mile drive to their house.

When we got to the house, my mom was there, which was a little confusing. And there was a strange quietness and feeling of something being off. I knew something was wrong but had no idea what it could be. I certainly wasn't expecting it to be a life-altering event that would affect us forever.

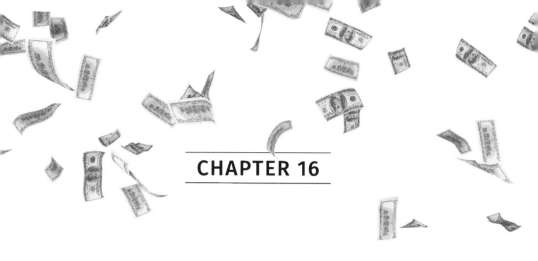

It wasn't long before I was told the reason that my uncle had brought me there instead of taking me home. My dad had died of a heart attack earlier that day at the young age of thirty-nine. WHAT?! I was numb at the news. It just couldn't be true. But it was. He had died on the way home from having his wisdom teeth pulled. My mom had been driving and my little brother was in the backseat. She looked over at him and noticed that my dad was pale. He was also cold to the touch. She pulled over. A driver passing by stopped to help and ran to a house nearby to call for help. My dad was already gone when the medics arrived.

I never got to say good-bye.

I will also never forget the day of the funeral. The church we attended was filled with people. I sat in the front row with my mom and the rest of my family. Because my dad was a decorated police officer, it seemed like the entire police department was there. I remember the casket. Afterward, I remember the burial and the gunshots going off and the folding of the flag. And as I sit here writing this and remembering all of it again, the tears are streaming down my face. When you lose someone you love, you never really get over it. You just take one step at a time and learn to move on because you don't really have any other choice.

Being a child, I didn't know anything about money or how something like this kind of tragedy could affect a family's financial situation. It would be many years later, when I was an adult, that I finally realized and understood the impacts.

First, we were very lucky that my dad had a life insurance policy. As he was a police officer, there was always a chance that he would die in the line of duty, and he wanted to make sure that his family was taken care of if that were to happen. We also had Social Security payments coming in. So, as far as I was aware initially, nothing much had changed. We didn't have to move and there was still food in the refrigerator. In fact, in some respects it often felt like we had *more.*

Within a year or so after my dad died, I started to feel this incredible sense of guilt. You see, after a while, we seemed to have more money and I was happy about that. The reason I knew we had more money was that my mom had added a large family room to the back of the house and a separate laundry room. We would never have been able to do that when my dad was alive. To me as a child, being happy that we had more money must mean that a part of me was happy that my dad had died. It was a terribly conflicted time. To deal with the loss of a parent and at the same time deal with guilt surrounding that loss is a lot for an adult to handle, much less a child.

No one in my family really talked much about my dad's death when I was growing up. It was too painful and it was always like the elephant in the room. But when I told my mom about this book and that I was writing a chapter about how Dad's death affected me, she started sharing some of her reflections. I found out she had felt guilty that we had more money too. She said that my dad loved cars and always wanted to buy a new one. My mom managed the money and would always tell him no, we couldn't afford one. After he died, my mom bought a new car at her dad's (my grandpa's) urging. She felt a lot of guilt that her beloved husband was never able to have that new car but she was. You can read more of her story at the end of this chapter.

Preparing for the Worst

Life throws us curveballs and crises. We can be sailing along with everything going great and then – wham! – something unexpected happens or some timeline gets moved up that you didn't plan for. It can be something simple, like the air conditioner that was on its last leg finally gives out in the middle of summer, or your car blows a tire on the highway. However, it might be something much more serious. You are in a serious car accident. Your son falls off his bike and breaks his arm. You or a spouse gets cancer. An older parent needs special care, so you have them move in with you. An immediate family member dies unexpectedly. Any one of these things can send you into an emotional and financial tailspin.

And have you noticed that you don't usually just experience one curveball or crisis? No, we usually have to face them multiple times. Sometimes, they happen within a short period of time or seem to come in rapid succession. In the fall of 2009, I was in a one-car accident in which I totaled my car and broke my left collarbone. A few months later, they checked and found that my collarbone was not healing and fusing on its own, so I had to go through my first-ever surgery and have a plate and screws put in. Then, a couple months after that, I fell down the steps at a friend's house and broke a bone on the side of my left foot. I was in a boot for about four weeks. All of those things happened within a matter of months. Each of them required physical recovery, time off work, and financial payments.

The medical bills during that time were ridiculous! Thankfully, I had good car and medical insurance that took care of a lot of them. I still had to pay quite a bit out of pocket, but when I looked at what the cost would have been without insurance, I about had a heart attack. No wonder people go into bankruptcy because of medical debt.

Aside from insurance, the other thing that really helped me was that I had accumulated some money in my emergency savings account (I had finally started that whole planning thing by this time). So, when those curveballs came along that year, I didn't have to stress or wonder how I was going to pay the bills. Okay, I still stressed, but it was because I didn't want to be dipping into my savings account for that reason.

These life events can happen anytime and anywhere. Although they sneak up on us and take us by surprise, we actually can plan for them. In this section, I share with you six policies that are critical to have as you prepare for your own curveballs and crises. Much of this information may not be news to you, but if you're like I was, there are at least one or two of them that you probably have a ways to go before you are fully protected.

Health Insurance

Most people have some type of health insurance, either through their employer or with an individual plan. Some people, however, think they don't need it because they are very healthy. Others don't have access to insurance at their workplace, and they choose not to get it from the Marketplace. It's one thing to not have insurance for yourself and your spouse, but if you have dependents, then you've got to have some health insurance. I know that paying for medical insurance can take a bite out of your budget. Still, you never know what can happen to you, your spouse, or your child. It will cost you a lot more money if one of you ends up in the hospital for some reason.

Medical expenses can quickly spiral out of control. Just going in for an annual exam can create havoc with the budget if you don't have the money up front to pay for the visit. But there are some ways to control these types of expenses. Maintaining a healthy lifestyle, by eating right and exercising regularly, is a key component. It's also important to go in for those periodic wellness and preventive exams because those can detect possible problems early, thereby saving you money in the future. Many employers have in-network doctors that they recommend you consult with. Going to someone that is out of the network can cost you more money.

Medications and prescriptions can become expensive, especially if you have a chronic medical condition. Even with insurance, the money needed for these can take up a sizable portion of your cash flow every month. See if you can get a generic brand or use a mail-order program if it's available.

Life Insurance

If you are married or have dependents, you absolutely need life insurance. You want to be able to provide for your family in the case of your death. Many people find this topic confusing and have lots of questions. I am not an authority in this area, but I can tell you what many of the experts recommend. (For more complete advice about your specific situation, talk to a trusted insurance agent to discuss your options.)

First, I have found that most financial experts who do not work in the insurance industry will tell you to buy term life insurance instead of whole life or cash value life insurance. The reason is that insurance and investing serve two different roles, so they should not be mixed (which is what whole life insurance does). Life insurance is to take care of your family in the event of your death, whereas investing is to take care of you in retirement. Whole life insurance can be complicated to understand, with various fees associated with it. I encourage you to do your research if you are thinking of purchasing this kind of insurance. Personally, I stick with term insurance.

There are various recommendations for how much life insurance you need depending on your life stage and age, for example. I'm not going to give you a recommendation. Just know that you probably want to be a little more liberal instead of conservative, and make sure that you get enough to cover living expenses for your spouse and dependents as well as enough to pay off the mortgage, funeral expenses, medical expenses, and any other outstanding debts.

If married, both of you should have life insurance, even if one doesn't receive an income. The reason to have some insurance on a nonworking spouse is that person undoubtedly takes care of many of the chores at home and may take care of the children if there are any. Upon that spouse's death, you will now be responsible for all of that and may need to hire help.

If you're single without anyone who depends on you to take care of them, you probably don't need life insurance. Remember, the purpose of life insurance is to provide financially for those immediate family members who have been left behind and counted on your income. Also, keep in mind that once your children are adults and on their own, they are no longer considered dependents. You should take this into consideration when determining length of time and the amount for your policy.

One last thing about children and life insurance. Whether to have a policy on a child is a debate in the financial and insurance industries. Some say you should carry a whole life policy and use it as a savings account to help pay for funeral expenses and medical costs. They also say that you should have a policy on your children so they can get a cheaper policy as an adult. Those on the other side of the debate argue that you should save enough in an emergency fund to cover this potentiality and that term insurance is still going to be very cheap when that child becomes a young adult.

Whichever choice you make, be sure you understand the policy that your insurance agent recommends for you. Don't be afraid to ask questions! Don't let them talk you into something that you don't understand or disagree with. It's okay to tell your agent that you need to think about it before making a decision and signing off on something.

A Will

Please read this section even if you are single with no dependents! Do you know that over half of Americans die without a will? If you own property or have assets, you need a will – a legal document that states what happens with these things when you die. I know, it's not something any of us likes to think about. But if you don't have a will in place, your state may determine who gets it. Is that what you want?

In full transparency, I fought creating a will for more than twenty-five years. Why did it take me so long? As a young adult fresh out of college, I didn't really have anything to leave anyone. Once I did have some assets, I started thinking that I should probably look into getting a will, but it just seemed like a lot of work. All the information that I saw about having to divide all your assets and name who gets what just seemed like a major headache, and I didn't have time for it. I also had no idea who to talk to and didn't want to pay the money for an attorney. Finally, I was in denial that anything would actually happen to me. You would think that having been in two major car accidents where I should have died would have scared me straight, but it didn't for another few years.

Something finally clicked. Maybe it was the fact that I owned my home and had some fairly significant assets. Maybe it was because I felt like a fraud because as a financial coach, I encourage everyone I talk with to have a will, yet I didn't have one of my own. Or maybe it was hearing about so many people who had died early and unexpectedly without a will and the problems that it created. The bottom line is that the control freak in me came out and convinced me that it was time to take control over my assets. I wanted to decide who was going to get what.

After finding an attorney to work with, the most challenging part was deciding who would get what. I actually canceled my first appointment when I was supposed to finalize and sign the document. And I came really close to canceling the second appointment. I kept overthinking and analyzing to the point that I was getting paralyzed in making a decision. In the end, I recognized that it was better to have a will that I wasn't 100% sure of than to have no will at all. That was something I had heard from various financial experts as well. I can always change it in the future if I want to.

As I mentioned earlier, if you die without a will (called intestate), your state may determine who gets your property and whatever assets do not have a beneficiary already named to them. The state will very rarely take your money. Instead it will find your living relatives and give it to them. There are several scenarios of what can happen depending on what family members you have living. For example, in Indiana, where I live, if you are married with children, your spouse would get half of the inheritance, and your children would get half. If you are single with no children, your parents would inherit everything; if you don't have parents living, your siblings or grandparents would inherit your assets. If you don't want a certain family member to get the bulk of your estate, you better have a will so you can name who does get it. You can find out more information about this by doing an Internet search for "dying without a will in [whatever your state you live in]."

Further, if you want to leave money to a church or charitable organization, you must have a will in place to do that. For example, I knew that I wanted a percentage of my assets to go to my church and a local animal shelter. I made sure to include both of those organizations in my will.

Note that having a will is not the same thing as having life insurance; you need both of them. A will is also not the same thing as having named a beneficiary to your 401(k) or 403(b) investment accounts. A will does not change or affect those decisions. Although it may sound confusing and like a lot of work, making a will doesn't have to be overly complicated. You just want to make sure that you get to control who inherits your property and assets that are not already designated to a beneficiary. Simple, right?

Home & Auto Insurance

Nearly everyone knows they need homeowner's or renter's insurance and auto insurance. It's simply another layer of protection for you and your assets. If your home catches fire or you get into a car accident, insurance steps in to help cover the resulting bills. How many times have you read about someone's home catching fire without any kind of warning? It happens all the time. If someone slips and falls on the ice on your driveway, you may need to cover that person's medical bills. If you hit someone else's car or person with your car, you are responsible for the damages and any injuries.

When shopping for insurance remember: you need enough to

cover total loss, but you don't want to have extras that you don't need. Go find your last statement and look at what types of coverage you are currently paying for. Go ahead, I'll wait. When you're ready, we'll discuss what you do and don't need.

Homeowner's Insurance. You want enough insurance to pay for a new home if necessary, to replace personal possessions and property in the home that could be lost in a fire, and to cover injuries that happen on your property. These are commonly referred to as dwelling, personal property, and liability. These are the three basic ones that all of us should have. There are other coverages that you might be paying for or want to include. For example, if you provide child care in your home, you would want the child care liability. If you run a business and keep product in your home, you will want extended coverage for that. If you live in an area prone to flooding, you will want flood insurance.

Most of us would have a hard time remembering everything we lost in the event of a total loss of our home, so I encourage you to take inventory of what you own. Write items down along with potential replacement value, or better yet take pictures, or videotape your rooms (much simpler). And don't forget your garage! Then, put your list, pictures, or videotape in a secure location, preferably not in your home.

Auto insurance. The cost and amount of auto insurance you need is based on where you live, what kind of car you drive, how many miles you put on it each year, and who drives the car. Before you buy a car, call your insurance agent to see what the projected monthly payments will be for that car. It will cost more for a teenager to drive, insurance for a sporty car is generally going to cost more than a sedan, and a brand-new car will cost more to insure than a used one. If you are on a tight budget, it is important to take this cost factor into consideration. You may have to choose a different car if the cost or monthly payment is going to sabotage your budget. Ideally, you should be paying cash for the car.

Legally, you need to be insured for yourself and anyone else who might drive your vehicle or be a passenger. The three main types of coverage that you need are liability, comprehensive, and collision. If you already have auto insurance, you wil see them broken out on your statement. Liability coverage takes care of property (car) damage and bodily injury as a result of an accident if you're found to be at fault. This coverage is a must, no matter what!

Comprehensive coverage is for damage resulting from pretty much anything that is not collision-related. A hail storm, a tree falling on your car, or even theft involving your car are all covered under the comprehensive part of an insurance plan. That leaves collision coverage, which kicks in when you hit another car or an object like a tree or fence. Unless your car is nearly worthless and you have money in savings to replace it if something were to happen to it, you probably need to keep collision coverage.

These three coverages are basic and necessary. There are other coverages that you may have or want. Some of these include uninsured/underinsured motorist coverage, rental reimbursement, and emergency or roadside assistance If you choose to pay for these coverages, just make sure you're not already paying for them elsewhere!

Another consideration when selecting an insurance plan is your deductible. The deductible is the amount you pay for repairs before the insurance kicks in. Many tend to go with a low deductible such as $250 or $500 because they know that in the event of an accident, they would only need to come up with that amount of money and insurance would take care of the rest. The downside is that a low deductible raises your premium (the amount you're paying monthly, bi-monthly, or annually). If you have a higher deductible, then you would pay lower premium. Choosing a higher deductible makes sense if you have enough savings to repair the vehicle in cases of minor damage. Because you are relatively unlikely to be in a major collision, you can save money each month with this plan. Bottom line: if you're not sure you can pay much out-of-pocket at the time of the occurrence, go with a lower deductible. You can check with your agent to see what the difference in cost would be if you wanted to change.

The amount of insurance you need for your home or car can change over time. Do a review every couple of years to make sure you're adequately covered.

Disability Insurance

This protection often gets overlooked and discounted as unimportant. The reality is that it is extremely important to have disability insurance. If anything were to happen (injury or illness) that caused you to be off work for a period of time, disability insurance would provide for *some* of the lost income. This could be the difference between weathering the storm and a major crisis that sends you back into debt and living paycheck to paycheck. There are two kinds of disability insurance that you can purchase: long term and short term.

Short-term disability (STD) is for when you have to be off work for up to about 12 months. It will typically cover 40%–60% of your regular income. For example, let's say you fall and break your hip and cannot go back to work for six months. Short-term disability insurance would kick in to take care of some of your lost income.

If you don't have any savings or have very little, you will want to have short-term disability insurance. However, once you have your minimum six to eight months of expenses saved in your emergency fund, you should be able to take care of a few months' lost income on your own.

Long-term disability (LTD) is for when you have to be off work for several months or even several years. You may start by using your short-term disability insurance and then have to take long-term. LTD typically covers 50%–70% of your income. Examples include injuries from accidents, cancer, brain injury, and some long-term mental health problems. You need long-term disability insurance, period. You just never know what will happen tomorrow that turns your world upside down and prevents you from doing your normal job, maybe for good.

You can usually get disability insurance from your workplace. Find out what the term of coverage is (how long can you be out of work) and how much the replacement income will be. If it's not enough to cover your basic needs, I encourage you to save up some extra money to cover the gap. Contact your human resources department to find out specific information about your coverage and what is available. If your employer does not offer disability insurance or you are self-employed, you should be able to talk with your insurance agent to get this type of coverage added. Again, only buy what you need.

Emergency Savings

The last "policy" I'm going to mention is intended for exactly what it says: Emergencies – those unexpected crises that happen at usually the worst possible times. This money is not for new furniture or landscaping supplies or any other want. It's not for an oil change or groceries or anything else that you should have planned for. It's for *emergencies*.

As I explained earlier in the book, you should start with around $1,000 in savings and work your way up to having three to six months' worth of expenses saved. My experience has been that six months makes people feel more confident, especially women. If you are single, have a one-income family, or have the majority of your income coming from an owned business, you should err on the high side. If you have a dual income or a very stable job, you might be able to get away with the lower amount.

There is one more type of insurance that I know some people might criticize me for not mentioning as necessary and that is long-term care (LTC) insurance, which provides for you when you need home health care or assistance with daily living activities as you get older. It can also help pay the expenses of assisted living or a nursing home. It is an important insurance to get, but whether *everyone* needs it is still very much up for debate. The reason I don't include it in the list here is that most experts will tell you that you don't really need to purchase it until you are in your fifties or sixties. So, although it's a great insurance to have, it may not be essential for you yet. Also, if you have a substantial amount in savings, you may not need this type of insurance at all.

Okay, so that was a lot of information. You might find yourself having glanced through it thinking it either doesn't apply to you or you already have it taken care of. If that's the case, please read through it again with an open mind. Remember, these are policies you should have in place to help alleviate the financial burden when curveballs and crises occur. If you don't have one of these in place or have been putting off getting it, I challenge you to do that now. Also, make sure you check the policies and documents you do have to make sure they are current and meet your family's needs.

At the beginning of this chapter, I shared with you how my dad's death affected me and that it was because he cared about his family that he made sure he had a life insurance policy in place in case something happened to him. Without it, I honestly don't know what would have happened to me and my mom and brother. Most of us don't believe a life-changing curveball is going to come at us, as if somehow we are invincible. Unfortunately, it just takes one unforeseen crisis to make us regret that way of thinking.

Now I am going to share my mom's story of losing her husband, my dad, when my brother and I were both young. I hope reading it will inspire you to take action to protect yourself and your loved ones.

My Mom's Story – Widowed with two young children (in her own words)

My husband was a police officer and while we were married our finances were definitely scarce. We lived payday to payday, and he worked two jobs to make ends meet. I wanted to wait until my children started school before I entered the work force. When my son began kindergarten, I began working at a local retail store. I was there for a year or so before a tragic thing happened to our family. My husband had a heart attack and died. It was so very hard to accept that this really happened and I kept asking Why?

Why? He was thirty-nine years old and my daughter was eleven and my son seven.

Thankfully, my husband had taken out a life insurance policy, which allowed our mortgage to be paid off. That helped us a great deal. I went to work in the school system as a teacher's assistant so I could be off when my children were off. When my daughter was ready for college, I started working at a medical clinic full time. Somehow, I was able to help her pay her way through college. I also helped my son with classes he took. They both received Social Security checks until age eighteen, so I had put money away for them and took out the necessary expenses like health insurance and whatever else they needed.

It was very hard emotionally losing my husband. I kept thinking, how are we going to survive without him? I really depended on my Lord, and I honestly feel He helped me raise my children.

I tried very hard to make a commitment to tithe as much as I could to my church by writing a check the first of every month. Everything I have is His.

-Judy Antrim

Spiritual Perspective

Every now and then, I run across someone who says they don't really think they need a certain kind of insurance because God will take care of everything. I agree that God is in control and will take care of us. But I also believe that He expects us to be wise with our money and protect our ourselves and our families in the event of a crisis. He also allows curveballs and crises in our lives. I'm sure you've experienced a few, as I have. It's a matter of being responsible and taking advantage of the resources God has provided us with to help us. If you don't think having one or more of these policies is important or it goes against your religious beliefs, then please make sure you have accumulated a large amount of savings to protect your family on your own if a crisis occurs.

Planning Your Escape

1. Have you heard a story or know someone (maybe even you) who was financially devastated because they didn't have one of the six components mentioned in this chapter? Describe that situation here:

2. Which policies do you need to finally initiate? Which ones do you need to check on or revise? Put a checkmark next to the ones you already have and are up to date. For those policies that need to be initiated, checked on, or revised, write the name of the person you will talk to next to the policy name and the date on the line for when you will have that done by.

   ____ Health Insurance
   ____ Life Insurance
   ____ A Will
   ____ Home Insurance
   ____ Auto Insurance
   ____ Disability Insurance
   ____ Emergency Savings

CHAPTER 17

Millennial Special

If you are a college student, a recent graduate, or in your young adult years and reading this book, thank you! I am so proud of you for taking the time and having the desire to stay out of the paycheck-to-paycheck conundrum. I wish I knew when I was your age what I know about money now and how my money story and experiences would impact my spending behaviors.

Here's what I want you to keep in mind: You don't have to follow the crowd; dare to be different! The crowd will spend too much, save too little, and get stuck in a well of debt. The crowd will run around in circles and be overwhelmed with financial stress. The crowd will keep looking backward and stop moving forward. You can choose a different path. The best time to do that is right now.

Do you want to have the ability to do what you want to do when you want to do it (a.k.a. financial freedom)? Then, do the opposite of everything that I did when I was your age! What does that mean? Well, you've got to avoid these easy-to-fall-into traps:

- **Buying too much too soon.** You get your first "real job" with a "real paycheck" and it feels like a lot of money. You decide to buy new clothes, a new car, move into an expensive apartment, or maybe even buy a house. Before you know it, you are spending more than you're bringing in. ***What to do instead:*** Be aware of your income and how much you can realistically afford without having to put it on a charge card; buy one or two new outfits instead of a whole new wardrobe and take it slowly; you don't have to buy everything all at once. Hold off on overspending on housing and instead find something that will meet your needs without costing half your paycheck; keep your car for as long as you can and when it's time for a new one, don't buy brand new. Even better, save enough money to pay cash for it.
- **Trying to impress other people.** You may feel pulled to keep up with the spending habits of your friends and co-workers. If you find you can't say no, you may have some decisions to make when it comes to the people you hang around with. Will you participate in the shopping spree? Will you go on vacation with them even though it will cost half a month's salary? Will you buy a car that is the same value or more than theirs so you look just as "successful"? ***What to do instead:*** Be aware of your emotions because that is what can get you into trouble and make you spend money without thinking through the consequences. Listen to the panicky voice inside your head that is telling you it's not a good idea to spend that

much money right now. It is critical that you decide early on to live *below* your income level. Try spending no more than 60%–70% of your income. I'm serious. This is how most millionaires get this status. They spend much less than they earn. The crowd doesn't believe this is possible because they don't make enough money. Hopefully, you remember what I said earlier in this book – it's not so much about how much you earn but what you do with what you earn! Bottom line: Live below your income and have a spending plan in place.

- **Not having an emergency fund that is just for emergencies.** As a young person, I was really good at putting money into savings but then would end up spending it on something like new furniture, a computer, or clothes. "Save to spend" is what that account was for. I never really thought much about emergencies or crises, and when I did think about them, I just told myself that I would figure it out when it happened. Of course, when a true emergency happened (and it always does), I didn't have the money to pay for it and was stressed about it. ***What to do instead:*** Understand what constitutes an emergency; keep a *minimum* of three to six months of expenses in this fund; and don't dip into it unless you truly have an emergency. Then, you can start those savings buckets for other higher-cost items you want. If you are a college student, think about a savings bucket for things like car repairs, gas money for going back home on the weekends, laundry money, and midnight snack runs.
- **Putting off student loan repayments or just paying the minimum amount due.** Millennials have some of the highest student loan debts in history. College tuition rates keep

rising and employment after graduation isn't paying what most graduates were expecting and planning for. You may have found yourself in a lower-paying job because you haven't been able to find one in your field of interest or you changed your mind and still don't know what you want to be when you grow up. That's okay, but your student loans will not go away. ***What to do instead:*** Create a plan to debt snowball your student loan debt. Looking at the total amount that you owe can feel like a really tall mountain that will take forever to climb up. And, I know you probably want to spend your money on activities that are a lot more fun. However, you really don't want to be in the position where you're still trying to pay off your student loans while trying to save money for your child's education. So, contribute as much extra money as you can every month to get them paid off as soon as possible.

- **Not investing in a Roth IRA as soon as you begin working and not investing in your company's retirement plan.** Truth be told, I did invest in a 401(k) through one of my jobs that I had early on, but upon leaving that job, I promptly cashed it in to pay for some debt-related expenses. Unfortunately, I didn't realize that in cashing out the 401(k), I wouldn't even get the full amount because I had to pay early withdrawal fees. And when it came time to do my taxes, I had a big wake-up call because I *owed* a bunch of money because the 401(k) money was considered income and I had to pay penalty fees! But the worst part came many years down the road when I realized the biggest mistake in doing this was that I lost the benefit of gaining compound interest, which would have meant FREE MONEY! ***What to do instead:*** If your employer has a 401(k) or 403(b) plan, sign up for it, especially if there is a company match. Too many people think they can't afford to have money taken out of their paycheck to be direct deposited into one of these plans or think that they don't need to start contributing until later. This is a *big* mistake that can cost you thousands of dollars! The earlier you start investing, the more time you have to allow compound interest to grow your money exponentially. If you don't have access to a retirement plan through your employer, then open up a Roth IRA account with a bank or financial advisor. Actually, you can do this even if you're contributing to a workplace retirement account, and if you have the extra money, I encourage you to do so. Don't wait to begin investing!

- **Playing credit card roulette.** This is when you start transferring credit card balances to other credit cards with lower interest rates or 0% financing because you can't pay your current balances. Eventually, it will catch up to you and your credit will be trashed. Trust me, because I've been there and done that! It sounds like such a great idea when you do it the first time or two. Yes, it may give you some temporary breathing room, but it doesn't fix the underlying problem which is that you have debt that needs to be paid off. ***What to do instead:*** Do not use credit cards! Most people spend much more money when they use a card (even a debit card) instead of cash. However, if you are going to use credit cards, make sure you pay them off in full every single month. Don't move the debt around and play games. Seriously, that's what you're doing – playing a game with your money. You will end up losing if you don't get this kind of behavior under control. In fact, don't even start it in the first place!

- **Failing to plan.** The majority of people fail to plan for the what-ifs in life. You can think that you'll never lose your fantastic job, have a medical crisis, or die at a young age. You can adopt the "I'll figure out how to pay for it later" mentality that your friends, family members, and coworkers have. You can go through life believing that you're not good enough, smart enough, or whatever enough. And the result will be that you end up stressed, overwhelmed, in debt, and maybe even alone. ***What to do instead:*** *Plan*! Set some goals. Set a timeline to get those student loans paid off. Create that spending plan (i.e., budget) that allows you to give, save, invest, and spend in a way that provides peace, security, and confidence. Get that emergency fund in place and start some savings buckets. Make sure you have enough health, home and life insurance in place. If you don't plan for the what-ifs in life, they will smack you in the face at the worst possible time. Ask your parents, grandparents, teachers, and mentors. They will gladly share their experiences with you.

The time to start your path towards financial independence is now, while you're young and can benefit from time and compound interest. I hope these tips have helped and inspire you to live a life different from those around you and most of the ones that are older than you. One that is debt-free, worry-free, guilt-free, and financially free. One that allows you to give and save passionately and abundantly. And one that will be a good model for your children to eventually adopt.

Let the crowd follow you!

CHAPTER 18

Solopreneur Special

If you own your own business or would like to one day, then you are part of an ever-growing group of people who are tired of the typical job where someone else controls your time and income. Most people are employed in a full-time career where they are paid hourly or by salary, and their pay is based on the number of hours that they are expected to work. The income is limited to hourly wages and salary caps. They're also accountable to a boss who evaluates their performance and decides whether they will get a raise or continue to even have that job.

These "traditional" jobs are still the norm and there is nothing wrong with having one of them. They provide structure, a sense of stability, usually some kind of health insurance, and often retirement options like a 401(k) or 403(b), among other benefits. High schools and colleges still primarily train students for a traditional kind of career, and parents encourage their children to pursue them as well. We need people in these jobs. Our way of life does not work without them. Can you imagine a world without educators, doctors, nurses, police officers, firefighters, attorneys, factory workers, restaurant workers, and a host of other careers?

Still, there are a number of individuals who are inclined to steer away from these types of jobs from the beginning. Others tire of working for someone else and decide they want to be in control of their own destiny. A few will start a business that becomes a large corporation or chain of stores that employs thousands of workers. More will run smaller businesses that employ dozens or even hundreds of workers. Others have a small family-owned business. And some – some are called solopreneurs: individuals who run their business by themselves or maybe have one or two part-time people that help them.

This chapter is devoted to these solopreneurs. Some examples include real estate agents, financial advisors, hair stylists, artists, musicians, coaches, bloggers, graphic designers, photographers, professional speakers, and online marketers. Those are just to name a few. These careers have become incredibly popular for a part-time or full-time income. Why? Mostly, it's the yearning for freedom. Solopreneurs don't have to report to anyone else. They don't have a limit on how much income they can bring in. And, they are able to work whenever and wherever they choose. It's what so many people say they want but are afraid to take the leap and the risk.

So, are you a full-time or part-time solopreneur? Even if you are not a solopreneur by definition, you may still want to read this chapter as it relates to money and running your business. Although self-employment brings many rewards, you also know the difficulties that it can bring. It can be lonely. It can be emotionally draining. It can be a struggle to constantly find enough clients and new business to generate the income stream you desire. It requires patience, persistence, organization, and motivation. Plus, you are responsible for finding your own insurance, which can be costly, and retirement strategies, which can be confusing.

Many solopreneurs (and entrepreneurs) are living the paycheck-to-paycheck lifestyle. They had this great idea of working for themselves and making a lot of money and then found it was a more difficult path than they had anticipated, due in part to the struggles you just read about in the previous paragraph. Does this sound familiar? If so, it's okay. We've all been there and had those times where we wondered if it was worth it and questioned if we should just give up. It's normal to think this way.

The rest of this chapter will focus on six strategies that can help you escape that paycheck-to-paycheck trap and become a more prosperous business owner. Keep in mind that this is a brief outline focused on how to help you create some systems so you are not running a paycheck-to-paycheck business. You are not going to find all your answers about how to run a business here. If you are just starting and need help figuring out how to do that, there are many other resources available (a few of which are in the Resources section in the back of the book). Okay, with that disclaimer out of the way, let's dive in!

Decide If You Have a Hobby or a Business

Your hobby can become a business, but your business should not be run as a hobby. If you want to make a few extra dollars here and there, it's cool, but that is called a hobby. You're doing it primarily for fun and as a way to spend some of your free time. The Internal Revenue Service defines a hobby as "an activity you engage in for sport or recreation, not to make a profit . . . even if you earn occasional income."[9]

The hobby vs. business question comes in to play most specifically when you are dealing with the IRS and taxes. (You are reporting your income on your tax return, right?) Different rules apply to a hobby compared to a business. Visit the IRS website to learn about the nine "tests" the government uses to determine whether your income is a business or a hobby. You may find it helpful, and you will definitely need to know which camp you're in when April 15 comes around.

But there is another side to this question and it has to do with your mindset. Here's the thing. If you're not bringing in the income that you want to, you may be treating your business more like a hobby. For example, hobby owners do not usually spend too much time on marketing their services because they are just doing it for fun. Business owners, on the other hand, spend a significant amount of time marketing because they need to continually find sources of revenue so they can create income and a profit. If you want to bring in an income you can live on, you will need to think more like a business owner.

So, do you want a hobby or a profit-making business? If it's a business, let's move forward with some more detailed strategies.

Create a Simple Business Plan

A business plan is essential for any business owner. It gives you and your business direction for the future. It doesn't have to be some complex official document, especially in the beginning. Make it simple. The best way to do that is to write it down, even if it's a few handwritten lines on a piece of paper. Your simple business plan should include the following components:

- *Mission statement* – Why does your business exist? What does your business do? Who is your target audience? What values do you focus on (speed, completeness, high quality, or customer service)? To get started thinking about this, you might start by completing this sentence: My business exists to _______________________. Consider adding your mission statement to your business card and other marketing materials.
- *Desired annual income* – Be realistic but challenge yourself. I want you to write down three incomes: (1) a baseline income, which is how much money you need to make; (2) a stretch income, which is how much you want to make; and (3) a dream income which, is one that would make you "giggle with glee." Your baseline should include all your business-related expenses as well as your desired salary. Your stretch income would challenge you to go beyond your comfort zone and allow you to have more abundance. Your dream income may make you very uncomfortable writing down but extremely excited to think about as a possibility. It is something you would work toward as your business becomes more established. This exercise is critical because if you don't know your income goals, you will have a hard time achieving the level of success that you're hoping for and may even end up with a loss at the end of the year.

- *Anticipated annual expenses* – Look back at last year's expenses to see if your costs will be similar or if you foresee any changes. Your expenses should include things like rent for office space, ink cartridges, and marketing supplies as well as payments that you make to a subcontractor or vendor. If your business involves purchasing inventory or having supplies available to create products, make sure you take all of that of into consideration. I recommend planning for more rather than less. Keep track of these expenses so you can claim them as deductions on your tax return. Also, don't forget to set money aside to pay taxes.
- *Action plan* – This is documentation of how you plan to generate your desired income. The easiest thing to do is divide your annual income by 12 to give yourself a monthly goal. If you have a side business and want to bring in $20,000, then that would be a little over $1,600 per month. Then, determine how you're going to bring in that money. How many clients would you need to have and at what pay rate? How many speaking engagements would you need to book and at what rate? How much product would you need to sell? Get the picture? You should also factor in how many hours you want to work and in what capacity. How many hours will you spend marketing, selling, networking, coaching, speaking, creating products, and so on?

If you have a seasonal business or one in which you tend to have predictable months with less income, then you might have to get a little more creative with your plan. Let's say your business is strong for nine months out of the year, and you have three months in which you bring in significantly less (they may or may not be consecutive months). You would need an income goal for those nine months and another one for the three months. Determine the *least* amount of income that you might generate in those three months (be conservative but not too much so). Then you can figure out how much you need to make during your more profitable nine months in order to reach your annual goal. The key is to make sure you are saving enough money from the profitable months to tide you over when you know you aren't going to have the income during the other months. I know of so many people who take a big salary from those great months and then have nothing to live on during those months when the income is scarce. Plan ahead!

- *Future goals* – Where do you want your business to be in three years, five years, and ten years? How will your business be different? Do you want to add employees? How long do you plan to keep the business going?

Once you have your simple business plan completed, keep it visible. You will probably find yourself revising it as you move through the year. Post your income goals, both monthly and annually, so you are aware of whether you are on track to meet your desired outcomes.

Have an Emergency Fund For Your Business

Just as you need a personal emergency fund, you also need one for your business. You may not have a business emergency per se, but chances are good that you will have some kind of unexpected expense come up. You want to be able to pay for it up front. I suggest doing it the same way as you would for your personal finances. Have a $1,000 starter fund initially and then work your way up to three to six months of business expenses depending on the size of your business. If you don't have a lot of expenses, your fund can be on the lower end. This will help keep you out of debt and can also be used during those lean months. Just remember to replenish it after you've dipped into it.

Develop a Working Budget

Remember when we talked about your money snapshot (a.k.a. budget or spending plan)? Well, I want you to do the same kind of thing with your business. Every month, you should be writing down your anticipated income along with your anticipated expenses (you figured those out when you did your business plan). You want to make sure that you will have enough money to cover your expenses and hopefully provide you with a salary every month. Save your receipts and track your expenses. You will be happy you did if you ever get audited by the IRS.

Run a Debt-Free Business

It is really easy to go into debt with your business, especially in the first few years. And most believe that it's a completely acceptable part of starting or running a business. But it doesn't have to be that way, especially for a solopreneur. Too many people don't think of saving money before they start their business or plan for the inevitable expenses that will go with it. Some businesses require very little start-up costs; others require inventory and other services to get off the ground. The problem is that we usually start buying more than what we really need. We attend every training or conference that is available, buy a lot of inventory, hire someone to create a website, purchase extra technology needs, and so forth. Be careful. Only buy what you need at first, generate some income, then you can buy some more later.

Keep in mind that not only do you typically spend more at the beginning of your business, but you also may not be taking much of a salary for possibly several months. You will want a cushion of money to fill the gap during those lean times.

You *can* run a debt-free business, and I strongly encourage it. You've just got to plan for it and be smart about your spending decisions.

Keep Your Finances Separate

It's really important that you keep your business finances separate from your personal money. You should have separate checking and savings accounts. In fact, I have my personal money in a totally different bank than my business money. If your business is a side job and you have a regular traditional job as well, it's easy to want to just combine everything. However, that co-mingling gets confusing. It makes it difficult to know how much money in the account is from your business and how much is from your other job. It also makes it much harder to do your taxes when everything is jumbled together. That is because you can't tell if you're using business money or personal money to pay for things. If you are serious about having a business, and not just a hobby, keep your monies separate.

However, even after you've separated your money, be careful about "robbing" one of the accounts. How many times have you used business money to pay for a personal item or personal money to pay for a business expense? Stop it! Simplify and keep it separated. If you *absolutely must* borrow for some kind of emergency, make sure you pay it back as soon as possible.

If you follow these six strategies, you will have a better chance of having a successful business. You won't have to worry about living paycheck to paycheck because you know how much income you need to bring in every month and you have money saved for unexpected expenses. I'm not saying you'll be super successful and won't have any problems. Obviously, I can't guarantee that. You still have to do the work and make the right choices more often than the wrong ones. But if you follow these principles, you will have a strong foundation on which to build your business.

Conclusion

I've met dozens of smart, hardworking, generous, and talented men and women who have finally decided that they are tired of living paycheck to paycheck. They are fed up with feeling stressed out all the time and wondering if they will have enough money to pay all the bills every month. They want money in their savings account. They want to be able to give more generously. And they want to be able to retire early enough to enjoy it. But, they wonder if it's just too late. Is there any hope to change their situation?

I hope that after having read this book, you agree that it's not too late and there is always hope. I've not promised that it will be easy. In fact, I'm pretty sure I told you it will be hard, right? Changing habits, priorities, and mindsets is not always fun, especially in the beginning. I remember trying to change my shopping habits and put the priority of saving money ahead of spending it. It didn't just happen over a month or two. It took time. And I failed . . . a lot. Eventually, with time and practice, I developed new habits and mindsets that continue to keep me focused on achieving my goals.

Don't give up! You will have good months in which you have money left over and you're feeling like things are finally looking up. And you will have those months when you wonder what happened. How did you go off track again? It's okay. Don't beat yourself up about it. Figure out what went wrong. Look back at all your expenses for that month and find out where the money went. Did you forget to plan for something, like your vehicle's registration fee or homeowner's association dues? It's easy to forget those expenses that don't occur every month. Did you spend more eating out that month because you were traveling or working longer hours? Did you splurge on some personal items? Or were you simply not keeping track of your expenses or not adhering to your budget? If you're like me, that last one is most likely what happened!

If you really want to change your financial situation and stop living paycheck to paycheck, you must create that awareness of what you're spending your money on. You need to have a spending plan, and you've got to stick to it. There are times when I have $10 left in my restaurant envelope and still have a week left to go for the month. If I'm serious about staying on my plan, I might be able to go out one more time. Mindset Alert: I do not see this as being restrictive or not being able to do what I want to do. Just the opposite, it allows me to stick to my plan and reach my ultimate goal. Usually, when I have only $10 left, it's because I wasn't planning and watching my cash the first three weeks.

As you start seeing positive changes in your financial situation, you may start having some of the I-wish-I-would-have and If-only thoughts as I did (and still do at times). "I wish I would have started saving and investing earlier." "If only I could redo my young adult years and not make all the mistakes that I did." "If only I hadn't spent so much money on stupid stuff in my twenties and thirties." "If only . . . I'd be so much better off than I am now." The reality is that I cannot change the past, and neither can you. You can choose to dwell on all the mistakes you made and be a victim to those negative thoughts or you can acknowledge them, embrace them as learning experiences, and keep moving forward one small step at a time.

It's time to escape the paycheck-to-paycheck trap. For yourself and for your family. Here are my final reminders to help you make that happen.

- Take your money snapshot and then create your monthly spending plan, where you tell your money exactly where you want it to go.
- Put money in your emergency fund and do not touch it unless you have a true emergency.
- Track *all* of your expenses, even that $1.50 that you put in the vending machine.
- Create your debt-snowball plan.
- Live below your means. That's the golden rule for attaining wealth.
- Keep your goals in mind when you are about to spend on something nonessential. Ask yourself, "Do I really need this, or would I rather have something else?" For example, "Do I really need this new seventy-inch television or would I rather be debt free?" Debt-free should be your answer!
- Think about your Why-What-How. Why is escaping the

paycheck-to-paycheck lifestyle and living debt free important to you? What will it allow you to do or be? How will you feel and how will it change your life and that of your family?

- Dream about and start preparing for the future when you will be able to give, save, and invest abundantly and spend without the guilt.

Remember, your income is often a secondary issue. The primary issues are usually lack of planning, inadequate savings, and spending beyond what you make. It becomes an income issue when those primary issues go out of control and you can no longer cover all of your expenses, let alone try to do the debt snowball process.

Here's the thing... you can do pretty much anything for a short period of time. Think about a painful time that you didn't think you'd get through, either physically or emotionally. It may have been a broken relationship, childbirth, a physical injury, or something else. You eventually got past the pain because it was short-lived.

Similarly, there are hundreds of stories of people who worked two jobs or stopped spending money on big family vacations for a few years so they could get their debt paid off and have extra cash flow. It wasn't fun for them; they might even say it was painful to be away from their family or have to say no to themselves or their kids when they wanted something. But the reward of being debt-free and having a supersized savings account made it all worth it to them in the end.

So, you have a choice to make. Are you going to continue to do what you've been doing for quite some time now? Or are you ready to escape that paycheck-to-paycheck trap once and for all? Are you willing to give up a little now so you can have a lot more later? I promise you it will be worth it. I've been on both sides, and although it was tough to change my spending habits and get out of debt, I love being debt-free and having the freedom to give abundantly and spend without guilt. If I can do it, so can you. You've got this!

I would love to hear from you. Please send your stories, comments or questions to tina@antrimfinancialcoaching.com

Good luck and God Bless!

Income Chart

Monthly Income #1:	$
Monthly Income #2:	$
Other Income:	$
Other Income:	$
Total Monthly Net Income:	**$**

Monthly Expenses Chart

Fixed Expenses		Discretionary Expenses	
Church/Charity	$	Groceries	$
Savings	$	Eating Out	$
Mortgage/Rent	$	Household Items	$
Car Payment 1	$	Personal Hygiene	$
Car Payment 2	$	Kids Expenses	$
Home Phone	$	Babysitting	$
Cell Phone	$	Clothes	$
Electricity	$	Vacation/Travel	$
Water	$	Pet Food/Supplies	$
Gas	$	Entertainment/Hobbies	$
Trash/Recycling	$	Dry Cleaning	$
Cable	$	Subscriptions	$
Internet	$	Memberships	$
Health Insurance	$	Blow Money	$
Life Insurance	$	Miscellaneous	$
Car Insurance	$	Other:	$
Medical	$	Other:	$
Tuition Payment	$		
Other:	$		
Other:	$		
Total Fixed Expenses:	$	Total Discretionary Expenses:	$

Debt Repayment Chart

Name of Debt	Minimum Payment
Credit Card #1:	$
Credit Card #2:	$
Credit Card #3:	$
Credit Card #4:	$
Credit Card #5:	$
Credit Card #6:	$
School Loan #1:	$
School Loan #2:	$
School Loan #3:	$
Medical Debt #1:	$
Medical Debt #2:	$
Line of Credit:	$
Personal Loan:	$
Other:	$
Other:	$
Total Debt Payments:	**$**

Nonmonthly Expense Chart

Expense	Amt Due	# Months	Mo. Pymt
Car Repairs			
Auto Insurance (non-monthly plan)			
Tuition Payment (non-monthly plan)			
Homeowners Insurance			
Property Taxes			
Holiday Expenses			
Other:			
Total Non-Monthly Expenses:			$

Total Monthly Net Income: $________________

Less Total Fixed Expenses: $________________

Balance (subtract #2 from #1): $________________

Less Total Discretionary Expenses: $________________

Balance (subtract #4 from #3): $________________

Less Total Debt Repayments: $________________

Balance (subtract #6 from #5): $________________

Less Total Non-Monthly Expenses: $________________

Final Balance (subtract #8 from #7): $________________

Debt Snowball Chart

Name of debt	Balance	Min Payment	Interest Rate
Total Debt Payments:	$	—-	—-

Write the extra monthly amount that you are going to add to snowball your debt:

$__________

Notes

Chapter 1

1. "Planning & Progress Study 2018," Northwestern Mutual, https://news.northwesternmutual.com/planning-and-progress-2018. Click on Money and Emotions
2. "Recession officially ended in June 2009," Chris Isidore, CNN Money, September 20, 2010, https://money.cnn.com/2010/09/20/news/economy/recession_over/index.htm

Chapter 2

3. "Living Paycheck to Paycheck is a Way of Life for Majority of U.S. Workers, According to New CareerBuilder Survey," CareerBuilder, Chicago and Atlanta, August 24, 2017, http://press.careerbuilder.com/2017-08-24-Living-Paycheck-to-Paycheck-is-a-Way-of-Life-for-Majority-of-U-S-Workers-According-to-New-CareerBuilder-Survey
4. "Paycheck to Paycheck," Julia Kagan, Investopedia, November 27, 2017, https://www.investopedia.com/terms/p/paycheck-to-paycheck.asp

Chapter 8

5. Karen McCall, *Financial Recovery* (Novato: New World Library, 2011), pp. 83-84.

Chapter 9

6. Charles Duhigg, *The Power of Habit* (New York: Random House Trade Paperbacks, 2012)
7. "Addiction: Substance Abuse", n.d., https://www.psychologytoday.com/us/basics/addiction

Chapter 15

8. Mary Hunt, *Smart Woman's Guide to Retirement Planning* (Grand Rapids: Revell, Baker Publishing Group, 2013)

Chapter 18

9. "Tax Tips for People Who Earn Income From a Hobby," n.d., https://www.irs.com/articles/tax-tips-people-who-earn-income-hobby

Resources

There are so many helpful resources out there that I could recommend. These are just a few that came to mind that I thought you might be interested in.

Websites and Blogs:

- Nerd Wallet: https://nerdwallet.com
- The Penny Hoarder: https://www.thepennyhoarder.com
- The Simple Dollar: https://www.thesimpledollar.com
- For savings accounts and mortgage comparisons: https://www.bankrate.com
- Budgeting Planners: https://www.everydollar.com

Debt Snowball Calculators:

- https://www.nerdwallet.com/blog/finance/debt-snowball-calculator/
- https://financialmentor.com/calculator/debt-snowball-calculator
- http://www.calcxml.com/calculators/restructuring-debt?skn=38

Books:

- Business Boutique by Christy Wright
- Debt-Proof Living by Mary Hunt
- Financial Recovery by Karen McCall
- Love Your Life Not Theirs by Rachel Cruze
- Money Making Mom by Crystal Paine
- Retire Inspired by Chris Hogan
- Smart Woman's Guide to Retirement Planning by Mary Hunt
- Start Late, Finish Rich by David Bach
- The Millionaire Next Door by Thomas J. Stanley and William D. Danko
- The Total Money Makeover by Dave Ramsey

Acknowledgments

I knew that writing a book would be a huge endeavor. But I didn't realize how much time and energy it would take and how many sleepless nights I would endure throughout the process. From my computer shutting down unexpectedly and losing several pages of material to feelings of inadequacy and anxiety, there were times I wanted to quit.

Thankfully, I had a small army of people in my corner who supported and encouraged me to keep going and another group of people that pushed me beyond my self-imposed limits and gave me the tools to get this book published.

First, I thank God for changing my life and blessing me with more than I could have dreamed.

The coaching team with Steve Harrison's Quantum Leap Program has been fantastic to work with. Special thanks to Raia King who helped get me started and Geoffrey Berwind who was instrumental in helping me figure out the title. Also, Martha Bullen who worked tirelessly with me the last few months by answering all of my questions, helping me make decisions, and keeping me on track. Martha, you were a godsend!

Katherine Pickett, my amazing editor, who took my book to the next level. Thank you for challenging me on some of the topics and giving me another viewpoint to consider. And for showing me how to properly use commas!

Jerry Dorris, for creating the fabulous cover and doing the interior design. I had absolutely no idea what I wanted done for the cover and gave you very little direction, but somehow you were able to come up with something I love and am proud of.

Eric Dubach and Amanda Rzicznek, for reviewing the preliminary manuscript and offering your thoughts and suggestions. Knowing that you both loved the book gave me the confidence to move forward.

My friends and family who often asked how the book was coming along and shared in my roller-coaster ride of excitement and fatigue. Although I would like to recognize all of you by name, I know that I would inevitably leave someone out and then I would feel terrible. You know who you are, and you have my deepest appreciation for your love and support.

My clients who have trusted me with their stories and allowed me the privilege to join them on their journey toward becoming debt-free and having financial freedom. You help me be a better coach and steward every day.

Judy Antrim, my wonderful mom who constantly shows me and everyone around her what a giving heart looks like. Thank you for your constant support and faith in me!

About the Author

TINA ANTRIM, M.S.Ed, BCC, is a speaker, author, and board-certified coach specializing in financial life coaching. As a former chronic spender, Tina knows what it's like to live paycheck to paycheck and feel overwhelmed with debt. She knows the guilt, shame, embarrassment, and fear that can paralyze and make us feel completely inadequate. She finally got sick and tired of not having any money left at the end of the month and decided to make some changes to her habits and mindsets around money. Today, she is completely debt-free and is well on her way to financial independence.

Tina's mission is to help individuals and families find the same confidence, security, and freedom that she has found. As a financial coach, she helps people change their behaviors around money by creating awareness, accountability, and focused intention. She loves seeing her clients' money stories change and seeing them discover a brighter financial future.

In addition to her financial coaching practice, Tina is also a high school counselor, which she has enjoyed doing for 24 years. She loves working with high school students and being a positive role model for them. And sometimes she even gets to talk with them about money!

Tina lives in Fort Wayne, Indiana.

To learn more about how you can work with Tina,
visit www.antrimfinancialcoaching.com.

Connect With Author

Tina Antrim

ANTRIM
Financial Coaching

Sign up for Tina's monthly
newsletter and receive her
Top 25 Money Tips as a free gift
www.antrimfinancialcoaching.com

Schedule a free personal or business
Financial Coaching Strategy Session at
www.antrimfinancialcoaching.com/coaching

Schedule Tina to speak at your next event at
www.antrimfinancialcoaching.com/speaking

40719236R10137

Made in the USA
Middletown, DE
02 April 2019